THE

ATTRACTIONAL

CHURCH

THE
ATTRACTIONAL
CHURCH

Growth Through a Refreshing, Relational,
and Relevant Church Experience

BILLY
HORNSBY

NEW YORK   BOSTON   NASHVILLE

Scriptures noted KJV are taken from the King James Version of the Bible.

Scriptures noted The Message are taken from The Message. Copyright © 1993, 1994, 1995, 1996, 2000, 2001, 2002. Used by permission of NavPress Publishing Group.

Scriptures noted NAB are taken from the *New American Bible with Revised New Testament and Revised Psalms* © 1991, 1986, 1970 Confraternity of Christian Doctrine, Washington, D.C., and are used by permission of the copyright owner. All rights reserved.

Scriptures noted NIV are taken from the HOLY BIBLE: NEW INTERNATIONAL VERSION®. Copyright © 1973, 1978, 1984 by International Bible Society. Used by permission of Zondervan Publishing House. All rights reserved.

Scriptures noted NKJV are taken from the NEW KING JAMES VERSION. Copyright © 1979, 1980, 1982, Thomas Nelson, Inc., Publishers.

Scriptures noted NLT are taken from the *Holy Bible*, New Living Translation, copyright © 1996, 2004. Used by permission of Tyndale House Publishers, Inc., Wheaton, Illinois 60189. All rights reserved.

FaithWords
Hachette Book Group
237 Park Avenue
New York, NY 10017

www.faithwords.com

Printed in the United States of America

First Edition: February 2011

10 9 8 7 6 5 4 3 2 1

FaithWords is a division of Hachette Book Group, Inc.
The FaithWords name and logo are trademarks of Hachette Book Group, Inc.

Library of Congress Cataloging-in-Publication Data

Hornsby, Billy.
  The attractional church : growth through a refreshing, relational, and relevant church experience / Billy Hornsby. — 1st ed.
      p. cm.
  Includes bibliographical references.
  ISBN 978-0-446-57214-9
  1. Church growth. I. Title.
  BV652.25.H67 2011
  254'.5—dc22

2010022311

To all pastors who labor to fulfill the call of God on their lives, to church planters launching out to fulfill their dreams to do something significant for God, and to our faithful Lord for His eternal mercy and grace toward us.

To Charlene, my wife who has been my inspiration.

To the Lead Team at ARC for their commitment to doing church in an excellent way.

Contents

Acknowledgments

John Bolin who worked with me on the original idea for this book and for his creative touch.

Lynnmarie Cooke for her very hard work editing the first copies.

My staff at ARC for helping me develop successful church planting systems that inspired this book.

Gayle Bennett for all her work editing and helping me with the final copy.

Maurilio Amorim and Shannon Litton at A-Group for believing in the project.

Troy Parker, for keeping it Biblical.

Joey Paul at FaithWords for his encouragement and acceptance of the book.

Peter Haas for many helpful insights.

THE

ATTRACTIONAL

CHURCH

Chapter One

A Model for Growth

God is up to something great that will change the way Americans look at church. It will impact your church, your family, and this country over the next ten years and beyond. Your children and future generations will be excited about what God is doing!

A growing movement of churches is offering people a refreshing, relational, and relevant church experience. Because of their ability to attract large numbers of people to their places of worship, these churches have been defined as *attractional.*

Attractional churches rekindle a love for the lost, the absent, and the unfulfilled among their members, while meeting people's needs and empowering them for ministry.

Is your church an attractional church? Is it refreshing, relational, and relevant? If not, how can it become that kind of church?

Your church can be *refreshing.* Like ice-cold lemonade for someone who has toiled in the hot summer sun, your church can revive parched souls and quench dry spirits. The attractional church is refreshing because people may drink deeply from the oasis of the Spirit.

Your church can be *relational.* Your church can be a place of loving and warm friendships where weekly handshakes and hugs are more than just polite gestures. They are indicative of real relationships based on the love of Christ.

Your church can be *relevant.* Relevance is the cornerstone of the attractional church. Attractional churches make sense and pass the "Who cares?" test. A relevant church's members believe their problems matter and expect biblical answers. The church ministries relate to members and their real issues.

A good word to summarize this refreshing, relational, and relevant church experience is *life-giving*.

For pastors, this could be just another book about how to do church. Or it could contain just the information you need to restore life to your church and your ministry.

In the pages of this book, I have tried to capture the hearts of the innovators who make up the lead team for ARC, the Association of Related Churches, of which I am currently president and which I helped cofound in September 2000. They are my friends, my heroes, and my coworkers in Christ who are planting dozens of attractional, life-giving churches around the United States every year. These are pastors who represent the very best of the ARC in their innovation, their passion for people, and their love for Christ.

The reputation, influence, and success of these churches make them models for effective local church ministry. A commitment to transformational thinking has given these churches explosive growth and great influence across the country and around the world. With these churches as case studies, we will explore the philosophy, the strategy, and the potential for growth and expansion that exists when their principles—those that bring refreshment, relationship, and relevance to dying churches—are followed.

You will learn some profound but easily implemented practices that attractional church pastors use to reach their cities for Christ. Every member of every church can experience life again in church…in the church that Jesus intended for the unsaved world.

What Is an Attractional Church?

Obviously the attractional church is attractive—so much so that these kinds of churches are growing at a record pace in the United States and around the world.

While a number of attractional churches are megachurches, their real success can be measured by the number of souls that come to Christ and the impact the church has on its community.

The attractional church model's unique philosophy of mission and message contributes to its efficacy.

Mission: The Field or the Barn?

The mission mind-set in the attractional church focuses on the harvest to be reached as much as bringing people into the building. Many limit their Christian experience to church services in the proverbial "barn" instead of the life of the church in the community or the harvest. And though I believe that the focus of the true attractional church should be in the field of harvest, I also know that any harvest left in the fields will be ruined over time. So there has to be a harvest and there has to be a barn in which to put it. Any good farmer knows the importance of the barn; we should too.

Attractional churches believe that the harvest exists in cultures that we need to penetrate. We need to establish incarnational ministries within those cultures and effectively gather the harvest into places of worship. This does not interfere with the relational connection of the converts within a given group. The attractional church never loses sight of the souls Christ died for and attempts to reach cultures that the church has neglected in the past. The attractional church engages cultures outside the four walls of the church building instead of withdrawing from the culture surrounding it.

Message: Relevant Biblical Communication

The attractional church tends to draw people to its Sunday services because of its attractive style and relevant approach to communicating the gospel. In most cases worship is contemporary, but it doesn't have to be. Services are fun and happy, and the people are friendly.

Theologically, the attractional church's messages are biblically based. Staff members make sure they know the "market" in the area, and they make subtle adjustments to be relevant to that culture. So the way the Bible is presented is influenced by the culture that is being reached. The difference is not in the content of the message but rather in the style of presenting it.

Practical application is a big part of the messages in the

attractional church. "What I want them to know" *and* "What I want
them to do" are huge elements in the pastor's presentation. It is
in the application of the message that missions and outreach are
encouraged. Ministers relate application to everyday issues such as
family, employment, and finances.

The attractional church offers a large variety of services to the
community. Eventually, with growth, its financial and human
resources can be a one-stop shop for nearly every need that a
member has. A thriving attractional church can be compared to a
large hospital with a facility and staff equipped to treat a vast array
of illness, from acute emergencies and routine surgeries to compli-
cated and chronic diseases.

Attractional vs. Vocational

Some denominational churches serve mostly their members and
have virtually no outreach program for the community around
them. These churches emphasize their buildings and family programs more than reaching the lost in their community and have
therefore, for the most part, stopped growing. I call this type of
church *vocational*. Why? These churches are not "attractive" to
the underchurched community. I've said that to be attractional
means that there are some attracting elements. Vocational churches
have few.

A vocational church is usually led by a leader/pastor who sees
his ministry primarily as a means of income for his family. Bottom
line, he enjoys the ministry as a vocation. He feels a strong suit-
ability to the work and approaches it as his career. He is trained to
lead a church, to teach his congregation, and to provide guidance
in the routine and rituals of church life. He learns to be a good
communicator, counselor, and leader. Being a pastor or a priest is
his vocation...his job.

This church is, for the most part, passive about the community
and inwardly focused. The church leaders make little or no effort
to reach the lost and hurting unless it is the family members of the
congregation that are lost and hurting. Numerical growth is not an
issue.

As one pastor told me, "We are a small church that is not grow-ing, and that's the way I like it." Again, for the most part these are denominational churches that have been around for a long time and have had several pastors. Vocational churches also include those that have become tired and dated as the congregation has grown older, and the church members are unwilling or unable to keep up with a fast-changing culture.

The vocational church still serves the purpose of ministry to its congregation by providing a place to attend a Sunday service and ceremonies like weddings and funerals. Vocational churches may not be attractional, but they do meet the needs of thousands of congregations around the nation.

Is the Attractional Church Missional?

There is a lot written today about the need for the local church to be both missional (go to them) and incarnational (be like Jesus to the hurting and lost.) Many churches fail in these two categories. The challenge is to introduce these concepts to the congregational members in a way that there is a high percentage of buy in. It is not always easy. The truth is that any church can be missional, develop people to be incarnational and attractional at the same time. The answer lies in who's responsible for this to happen.

Many of the commandments of Jesus, like those in the Sermon on the Mount, were to the individuals who wanted to follow Jesus. Others were to the "Church" as a whole. So, without overstating this, I would like to consider the following as it relates to responsi-bility for being missional and incarnational.

Being "missional" is an individual responsibility—each of us must accept the responsibility to share Christ with others in any given situation.

Being "incarnational" is an individual responsibility—our trans-formation into the image of Christ by the renewing of our minds cannot be dictated from the pulpit but must come as a desire from within. Biblical instruction is necessary here.

Being "attractional" is a corporate responsibility—the leadership of the local church has the responsibility to present Christ and His

Kingdom as perfectly as possible the way it is revealed in scripture. It also must encourage and train its members to live as "sent ones," (living missionally) and to be like Christ (incarnational) to the lost world around them.

When all three concepts are fully embraced by the local church, then the more effective it will be in reaching the underchurched people around it.

Why Do We Need More Attractional Churches?

It doesn't seem that church—at least the way we Americans have been doing it—is working anymore.

In the book, *The American Church in Crisis*, author David Olson found that though 40–47 percent of Americans *say* they attend church regularly, it's just not true. After tracking 200,000 churches in more than 3,100 counties of the United States, he found that only 9.1 percent of Americans actually attend an evangelical church. This includes Pentecostal and charismatic churches. Only 3 percent attend a mainline denomination such as Lutheran or Presbyterian, and 5.3 percent attend a Catholic church. All told, 17.4 percent of Americans attend church on a regular basis, 23 percent "participate" in church, and 77 percent do not actively participate in any church, despite what they claim to believe about Christianity.[1]

According to the Barna Group, the average attendance in the average Protestant church in America is less than 90 people. Even worse, we're dealing with a population that is increasingly skeptical about organized religion. Only 52 percent expressed any confidence in organized religion, down from 68 percent in 1975.[2]

Quite simply, the boat is on fire and we need all hands on deck. If we don't dramatically refocus our efforts on souls, then we will tragically miss God's call on us for our generation. It's time to find a life-giving way to reach every lost person.

Now imagine if your child were stuck in a burning car. I doubt that you'd stand on the sidelines, wringing your hands. You'd be desperately seeking help. Your priorities would dramatically change. Based on the evidence, this is a suitable analogy for the state of the American church—it's in flames. And if we think that

God is pleased with our feeble attempts to do church while His lost children cry out for help, we are sorely mistaken.

God's sheep are in trouble, and we must rescue them. And we must learn from those who are demonstrating a special ability to do this.

Failures of the U.S. Church

The hard truth is that we have largely failed to reach the lost, the absent, and the unfulfilled—those I call the *underchurched*. We have failed to grow our churches with young innovative leaders. America's best innovators have become Internet entrepreneurs and computer game software developers. We've looked to politicians and self-help gurus to be our teachers and motivators and have allowed the gospel of Christ to take second or third place as our instruction manual for life.

That is why the average church in the United States has only eighty-five members. Most Americans have lost hope that the church can provide relevant help or answers to modern-day dilemmas. And faithful people are hoping desperately that someone will restore life to the local church.

Statistics tell us that approximately 83 percent of adults in the United States are staying home on the weekends—that's more than 250,000,000 people in the United States who don't attend church, or at least not very often.[3] It's not because they don't want anything to do with God; it is because they don't want anything to do with what they perceive as organized religion. God is great; it's just church they can't relate to.

The Lost

The lost are people who have not stepped across the line of faith to acknowledge the lordship of Jesus. When Americans are asked about their faith, they generally respond that they have some religious belief. However, when taking a different approach and analyzing respondents' answers to three questions that most evangelical leaders would say are core evangelical doctrine, only

22 percent of Americans fit the description of an evangelical in Gallup's May 2–5 poll.[4]

The Absent

The absent are those who know Christ but have stopped attending church services because doing so doesn't engage them anymore. As I mentioned, some 90 percent of Americans stay home on Sunday.

People are inundated with work, school, family, and recreational activities. With so much to do, they find it hard to set aside time to get involved in church. The distractions of the world are too overwhelming, and they just disconnect. With numerous activities to compete for our attention, we are making choices on how we are spending our time. And for *the absent*, these choices do not include church.

Author Dr. Richard Swenson writes in his book *The Overload Syndrome* that "the average American work-week now exceeds just about every other nation on the planet. Most homes are dual income with a combined total workload exceeding 90.5 hours/week," leaving very little time for family or religious activities.[5]

The main reason for these people's absence is that church is not relevant to their lifestyle. Many were raised in church, but once they were able to make their own choices, church was the last thing they would choose.

The Unfulfilled

There is a command from Christ and an expectation from our members that pastors should feed the sheep. Therefore, pastors devote hours to study and research ways to "bring the Word" on Sunday. Sheep get fed and thereby are happy. Right? Not necessarily so.

Of those who know Christ and attend church regularly, a majority still are unfulfilled and unhappy; as I mentioned in previous pages, 73 percent of Americans are skeptical of organized religion.

The unfulfilled attend church but don't engage in evangelism or other Christian service because they are bored. New, expanding suburbs are filled with people who have left their previous churches and never bothered to reconnect. Spiritually starved, they lack the nourishment they need to grow—let alone to help others. Sunday after Sunday, these devoted and committed Christians are hungry for something more.

Furthermore, they never bring friends, family, or other acquaintances to church because it does not seem relevant or life-changing. They leave church having heard more, learned less, unchanged, and troubled by the same problems as when they walked in.

So what really satisfies a hungry heart? What are we as Christians most hungry *for*? If a sermon does not engage our hearts or challenge us to follow Christ and bring the lost to Him, we will ask, *Why am I here, anyway? What is my takeaway for the rest of the week?* What needs to happen to ignite our passion again?

We need churches with life-impacting services and ministry. Now let us explore exactly how to do this. We'll study examples of wildly fruitful churches that are pulling in the lost, the absent, and the unfulfilled as never before.

A Successful Network of Growing Churches

The Association of Related Churches (ARC) started with a small team of great leaders and the vision to plant churches that would reach the underchurched in relevant, life-giving ways. As of this printing, the ARC has planted more than two hundred attractional churches.

Earlier I mentioned the word *life-giving* to connote a refreshing, relational, and relevant approach to ministry. I love that idea! In fact, most attractional churches have adopted that same terminology/philosophy in the way they do church. You'll see the term *life-giving* throughout this book to describe healthy, growing churches like the ones in the ARC.

What's incredible is that since the first ARC churches were planted in 2001, 90 percent of them continue today and most are growing. That is in contrast to most church-planting efforts in the past that have had only a 68 percent four-year survival rate.[6] What is even more remarkable is that some of these churches have reached Sunday attendance of more than seven thousand, with one particular church hosting more than fourteen thousand attendees on a regular basis. Nearly all of the ARC churches give 10 percent of their income to world missons, which adds up to over $7.5 million each year.

Making Your Church Grow

Is your church ready for a change? Is your church languishing? Maybe your church numbers are fine, but you sense your congregation needs a boost. Or are you launching a brand-new church and looking for practical help to begin your ministry the right way?

This book will help you navigate all these scenarios. We'll study the successes of thriving attractional churches as models to replicate, offering practical tips and methods you can implement right away. We'll help you take your church to the next level.

Be assured that your church—whatever its size, denomination, location, or current state—can grow. Your church can be refreshing, relational, and relevant.

Your church can be an attractional church.

PART ONE

Becoming an Attractional Church

Chapter Two

The Calling of Your Church

My wife, Charlene, and I spent eight years living in Mount Pleasant, South Carolina. Our years there were some of the best of our lives. Of course, the relationships we formed there are the lasting gems, but the beauty of the Carolinas simply cannot be forgotten. I know what James Taylor meant when he wrote "Carolina in My Mind." Charlene and I spent countless Sundays driving in the country. We loved the beauty of the marsh and the smell of the salt that swept in from the Atlantic Ocean. The mountains and the coastline are as idyllic as they are picturesque. But I have to tell you that my favorite feature of Mount Pleasant is the bridge that spans the colonial city of Charleston and the town of Mount Pleasant.

From atop this bridge you can see downtown Charleston, Fort Sumter, and usually dozens of boats scattered in the waters of Charleston Harbor. Driving on the bridge, you're likely to see sailboats gliding on the water, fishing boats heading out with hopes of making the big catch, and families enjoying a day on the water. Then there are the huge cargo ships and barges carrying goods from around the world. Of course, there is one boat that always stands out. Moored at the now famous Patriots Point is a hulk of steel that represents the very best of the American Navy. When you cross the bridge, it's impossible to miss an incredible boat called the USS *Yorktown*.

The *Yorktown* is a World War II–era aircraft carrier. It is the size of three football fields placed end to end. It weighs 27,000 tons and carried an amazing 2,600 officers and enlisted men. After serving the U.S. military for decades, the *Yorktown* was decommissioned and parked permanently at Patriots Point. Now, the magnificent boat has been transformed to a floating museum of U.S. maritime history. I have walked the decks of this boat, and it is every bit as impressive on the inside as it is on the outside.

The multiple decks of the *Yorktown* could carry up to 100 aircraft, which were propelled off the flight deck with massive catapults. There are 95 separate gun turrets designed to protect the airmen and the ship itself. Inside the ship there are sleeping quarters, numerous mess halls, and a galley with room to serve 2,600 people. Walking through the *Yorktown*, I couldn't help but sense the power and influence of this incredible ship. This ship alone could do great damage to the enemy, in itself a force to be reckoned with when encountered by enemy ships.

As I toured the *Yorktown*, I heard stories of great battles and near misses and incredible triumphs. I remember seeing a picture taken from the air of the *Yorktown* in the Pacific Ocean. The interesting thing was that the massive aircraft carrier never traveled alone on a mission, but always with at least a few other boats and most of the time as part of the entire Pacific Fleet. That fleet was made up of 9 battleships, 3 aircraft carriers, 12 heavy cruisers, 8 light cruisers, 50 destroyers, 33 submarines, and 100 patrol bombers. Naval military strategy is very intentional, and every boat in the armada has a specific purpose and function. Without each boat performing its function, the mission could be lost.

This was the case on numerous occasions such as the battles in the Marshall Islands where the *Yorktown* faced unrelenting attacks from Japanese kamikaze pilots. Without the destroyers and other gunships, the *Yorktown* would have been long lost. As important as the *Yorktown* was, the remaining fleet was every bit as important.

The Church Fleet

Mark 4:36 says of the disciples and Jesus, "and having led away the multitude, they take him up as he was in the boat, and *other little boats* were also with him." (Young's Literal Translation, emphasis added.)

We'll call it the Galilean Fleet. Instead of gunships, think of fishing boats. In the place of the USS *Yorktown*, we'll opt for the *Zebedee Cruiser*, courtesy of Peter and James's father. The Bible tells us that Jesus traveled by boat often, which was one of the fastest means of transportation in His day. It's interesting to me that Jesus didn't travel alone. Certainly, Peter's fishing boat would have been big enough to carry the twelve men. After all, the Gospels give us several accounts that place all the disciples together with Jesus in a boat. More than likely, Jesus was with His twelve disciples on the day described in Mark 4:36.

Jesus could have gone alone with His disciples across the sea, but that wasn't His style. In fact, He could have flown away on His own private jet or He could have chosen to stay home, content with being the big shot. To be sure, He was the biggest thing to ever step foot on that beach (or on the water, for that matter).

But look at that one phrase at the end of the verse: "other little boats."

It may seem like an author's afterthought, but I think these words speak volumes about the way God uses His church. The bottom line: It takes all kinds of churches working together to carry out an effective campaign against the enemy. Big ships and little ships can accomplish greater tasks together than a single vessel could accomplish alone.

Every Boat Is Important

God loves the big boats. When I think of Saddleback Church and Rick Warren's P.E.A.C.E. Plan...or Willow Creek's association of 12,000 churches that span the globe...or Thomas Road Baptist Church in Lynchburg, Virginia, with its 11,300 students at Liberty University and 900 churches in Liberty Baptist Fellowship...I know that God loves them.

But God loves the little boats just as much. Churches like Next Level Church in Fort Myers, Florida, and its pastor, Matt Keller, tirelessly serve church planters in the ARC. Next Level Church is growing as God is adding many to this congregation each year. And then there's Pastor Craig Wendel at SouthPoint Church in Southaven,

Mississippi; and Mosaic Church in Charlotte, North Carolina, where Pastor Naeem Fazal, a converted Muslim, is reaching hundreds of underchurched people. The list goes on and on. These churches are making a huge difference, and God smiles upon each and every one. Yes, He loves the big boats and the little boats too.

Maybe you're the pastor of a megachurch packed with thousands. Without a doubt, a big ship can do incredible things. With greater resources, it can give more to missions, help more hurting people, and accommodate greater numbers in weekly worship experiences. That said, we cannot ignore the unmistakable value of small churches, rural congregations, and new church plants. Don't forget that the smaller churches around you are a vital part of God's own fleet.

Are You the Pastor of a "Little Boat"?

Maybe you're the pastor of a small and struggling congregation and you've given up hope of ever growing past a plateau. It is the task of every church, not just the big ones, to make disciples and rescue people in desperate need of God.

Jim Graff of Significant Church Network shares the following statistics about the "little boats" in the United States:

- 6 percent of Americans who attend church attend megachurches.
- 34 percent attend churches between 300 and 2,000.
- 60 percent of people attend churches under 300 people.
- 88 percent of America's counties and parishes are under 150,000 people.
- 90 million Americans live in these counties.
- There are only 12 nations in the world with over 90 million people.
- There are 3,142 counties across America.
- 359 counties have more than 150,000 people.
- 2,783 counties have fewer than 150,000 people.
- 71 cities in the United States have more than 1 million people.
- 734 cities have between 50,000 and 1 million people.[1]

As you can see from these statistics, little churches are every bit as needed and important as the big ones are.

Speaking of boats, remember that it was Jesus' first commandment to His disciples to become "fishers of men" (Matt. 4:19 KJV). He knew that these men understood the fishing trade. He knew that they understood how boats and fishermen could work together to accomplish a task, so He used an example that He knew would stick: He encouraged them to become fishers of men.

Isn't that really the one thing we all have in common, regardless of our size or location or the composition of our congregations? No matter how big we get, we must never forget that everything we do inside our churches is designed for everyone outside our churches. At the same time, if we are in a smaller congregation, we simply can't rely on the "big guys" to get the work done. After all, Jesus didn't selectively pick the ones to whom He gave the Great Commission. Rather, as He ascended to heaven, He essentially looked at us all and said, "I'm going now, so you take My place. You can be My disciples. You can all become fishers of men" (see Matt. 28:19–20).

He didn't say those words only to the rich churches or the popular pastors or the articulate Christians. He spoke to every one of us who carry the name of Jesus. We all are charged with the same mission to know Jesus and to make Him known. So, if you've been holding back because of fear of failure, remember that a ship is safe in the harbor, but that's not what ships are made for. Or, as Jesus told His disciples, you are fishermen with boats, and your job is to fish. Therefore, fish.

As the Association of Related Churches plants more and more churches, we are discovering the contribution of each one, large and small. Each is a resource for world missions, a center for evangelism, a school of ministry and discipleship, and a coach to the next church planter when he needs a voice of experience. In God's economy, every church is valuable and filled with potential to do great things for Him.

Consider what some of these churches have accomplished in just a few years.

The journey of Wayne Hanson and Summit Church of Castle Rock has been an amazing story. In the first twenty-three months of the planting phase, nearly three hundred people have made commitments to Christ. A solid congregation of more than two hundred people call Summit Church home. Castle Rock, Colorado, is one of the most unchurched areas of the country, but God has given Summit Church incredible favor with lost people. Even after facing multiple weekends of blizzard conditions, venue changes, and an environment sometimes hostile to the gospel, Summit Church is not only growing, it is flourishing.

David and Ginelle Payne had a vision to plant a church in the heart of Massachusetts—an area not known for growing churches. Committed to the vision of God and convinced of the power of the fleet, Pastors David and Ginelle connected with the ARC and planted Lifesong Church in the heart of Worcester. In its first official service, Lifesong Church welcomed 394—the formerly churched, the disenfranchised, and the underchurched alike. It was everything the Paynes had prayed for. During the balance of that year, Lifesong experienced ongoing attendance of 219 on average. Dozens of people have made commitments and recommitments to Christ.

Bayside Community Church is a life-giving church with a goal of creating a sense of community in the Sarasota-Bradenton area of Florida. Pastor Randy Bezet and his wife, Amy, planted Bayside six years ago, and the church has already grown to more than three thousand in attendance. In just a short time, God has brought together an incredible team to express His love through practical ways such as community outreaches and missions projects of every kind. Bayside also takes an active role in holiday seasons by caring for needy families in the community.

Servant evangelism is an important part of ministry at Bayside. It exists to show the love of God in practical ways: washing cars, giving away school supplies, helping families and college students move into new homes or dorms, and freely offering everything from candy on Valentine's Day to cold drinks on a hot afternoon.

In his mid-twenties, Peter Haas found himself the senior pastor of a rural church in transition. After praying and fasting, he and his wife, Carolyn, were convicted that it was God's call for them to plant a relevant, life-giving church in the heart of Minneapolis. Substance Church was born with the intent to provide a place where underchurched people could connect with God and one another in a real and refreshing way. Emphasizing the importance of "doing life together," Substance has become a vibrant, growing church. Today, more than two thousand people attend services every weekend.

In each case noted above, the pastors understood the importance and influence of the leading-edge megachurches and learned to study and replicate their best practices—but they also understood the power of the fleet. They didn't start as big ships, but by God's grace and a commitment to reach the underchurched, they are making big waves in God's kingdom.

The Great Commission

Jesus came and spoke to them, saying, "All authority has been given to Me in heaven and on earth. Go therefore and make disciples of all the nations, baptizing them in the name of the Father and of the Son and of the Holy Spirit, teaching them to observe all things that I have commanded you; and lo, I am with you always, even to the end of the age." Amen (Matthew 28:18–20, NKJV).

How much do you think about these words? Do you realize the significance of "Go therefore and make disciples of all the nations" for your church? The importance that you place on these words will determine how your church members live their lives, which church the underchurched choose, how you as the pastor/leader will "do" church, and, ultimately, the eternal rewards you and your church members will receive from Jesus.

As followers of Jesus, the lives of your church members have so much meaning when they dwell on all that Jesus wants them to do—and then go out and do it. The Great Commission is one of those undeniable commands from Jesus that give us a peek into the divine will. If you are wondering, *What does God want my church to do?* ask no more. It is clear: *Go.* How and where your people go will ultimately determine with whom they share Christ and whom they disciple, but the answer is always to *go.*

This calling begins with you. You have to take it seriously and know He is talking to *you* first. Settle in your heart that you will be an example to your church as an ambassador of Christ wherever you go. I don't believe Jesus is *asking* us to go; He is *telling* us to go. So don't be satisfied with a vocational kind of service; ask rather that you would catch a vision and a passion for making your church attractional.

The underchurched all have in common the potential to be great missionaries for the cause of Christ. Each of us has a calling to reach people who will in turn reach others. I counted all the family members and their in-laws who came to Christ as a result of my conversion. I stopped counting at around 120 people. The potential to reach those people was in me, put there by God, long before I was saved.

The truth is that the potential in the people around us for fulfilling the Great Commission is huge—and *we've* got to be the catalyst. Some will reach folks in small towns, others will move to different cities across the United States, and still others will go to foreign lands to share Jesus. The results could surprise you. It starts with you.

The Sent Ones

Henry Nott was one of the first missionaries sent out by the London Missionary Society. Nott, a bricklayer by trade, arrived in Tahiti aboard the mission ship *Duff* in 1797. The mission did not prepare him or his fellow missionaries well for their situation in Tahiti. Our modern idea of the island paradise did not exist in 1797. The island was in a constant state of war. It was a barbarous place of the worst kind. It was ruled by an evil king named Pomare. This evil king was estimated to have killed two thousand people and sacrificed them to his idols.

The Tahitians burned their defeated enemies' homes, killing everyone in the villages. Children were sacrificed by being thrown alive to the sharks in the sea or into the fiery craters of volcanoes. These were the people to whom God sent Henry Nott. The people of Tahiti were heathens completely devoid of any decency, morals, compassion, or love. Yet, Nott knew that Jesus Christ died for these people and that they needed to know the love of Christ.

A year after it had landed, the *Duff* returned to England. Then, when it was loaded with supplies and on its way back to Tahiti, it was taken by a French privateer, the Buonaparte, to Montevideo, Uruguay. (Britain and France were at war during the reign of Napoleon.)

During the five-year wait for resupply, in Tahiti, several of Nott's fellow missionaries deserted the group, died, or seemed to go mad. Two of Nott's fellow missionaries were murdered and several abandoned their mission work and went into the trading business. He was left alone, but he knew his calling was sure.

Nott did not see his first convert until he had been in Tahiti twenty-two years—and that new believer was the heir to the throne. On May 19, 1819, Nott baptized Pomare II. In a short time, laws were passed that forbade the cruel murders. The islands were at peace. Nott returned to England only two times during forty-seven years overseas and was the primary translator of the Bible into the Tahitian language.[2]

Our calling may not be as sacrificial and demanding as Henry Nott's, but we are called nevertheless.

Some would argue that when Jesus gave the Great Commission, He was talking privately to His disciples. I must disagree. Look at the scope of what Jesus said: "Make disciples of all the nations" (Matt. 28:19 NKJV). All the nations! How could the remaining disciples accomplish this with no help? Their world had no public transportation like buses, trains, automobiles, or airplanes. Travel was all by tent and tote, step after step.

There was no Internet, no cell phones, no fax machines, and not one computer for another two thousand years. But even to date, with more than three hundred thousand churches in the United States,[3] millions of Christians and all the technology imaginable, fewer than 20 percent of Americans attend church on Sunday.

The Great Commission is our call to reach the world for Christ and make disciples of all nations. The underchurched world needs Christ, and the church needs to take action to reach them. That is why churches should be attractional—so the lost, the absent, and the unfulfilled can become disciples—and in turn make other disciples.

Chapter Three

The Showroom Floor

On the launch of EQUIP's Million Leaders Mandate initiative in Europe, Dr. John C. Maxwell's non-profit organization that trains leaders around the world, I was taking a walk with Dr. Maxwell, and several others. We happened upon a Rolls-Royce dealership. What happened next transformed my thinking about how to do church.

As we walked into the dealership, I noticed several paintings and posters that communicated the history and quality of the Rolls-Royce engine. The environment was not just comfortable but luxurious. I felt important, almost as if I could attain so great a status symbol (in my dreams). A beautiful Silver Cloud stood on one side of the showroom, inviting me to come and sit for a while. It was welcoming, just like the salesmen in the room. It was daring me to try it on for size.

Well, I did; I tried it on and in my own mind, it fit! When I closed the doors, it was like closing the door of a bank vault. I settled into the plush seat and never wanted to leave. But of course, it was not to be. I knew I needed to leave the dream and return to my real life.

But as we started to go, I had a provoking thought. If only I had that Silver Cloud, my life would be amazing. I was not ready to buy, but I was ready to ride!

And then it struck me: Why can't people walk out of church thinking, *If I had that, my life would be so much better*? Why can't we create an environment that knocks the socks off every person who comes through the door? Why not surprise them with excellence and excitement?

Well, why not? Why can't church services warm the heart, challenge conventional, secular thinking, and leave people with the sense that they've stumbled upon something wonderful? They may not be ready to "buy it" the first time around, but they may agree to "test-drive" the church a few more Sundays. Then one day they might settle in and make church their home and find Christ in all His glory.

I also have experienced high-pressure salesmen who tried to "close me" on their product way before I was ready to buy. I actually have left dealerships feeling like prey instead of a valued customer. I vowed never to return to those dealerships, and I never did.

What should your dealership (your local church) look like to entice the "customer" to want to return? Let's look at some ideas here.

Your "Dealership"

The Manufacturer: Jesus

It's critical to understand that Jesus is not the product. He is the Creator of the product, which is His church and His movement. He does not need the church, but He has chosen to use it to spread His message of hope and salvation. Therefore, He works in and through the church to empower and anoint His people to evangelize and disciple all who come to Him.

It's also important to clarify that when I refer to "the church," I don't necessarily mean the physical structure or a particular group; I'm talking about the whole body of Christ, the collective believers from every nation, tribe, and tongue who profess the lordship of Jesus Christ. They may or may not assemble in local congregations, but they are still His body. He created the church.

The Product: Christianity

We do not sell Jesus; He is not for sale. We represent Him in our worship and lifestyle. Our worship and lifestyle lead people either to Him or away from Him. We should reveal Christianity in a way that is appealing to the underchurched people of our community. Then we can lead them to Christ when they open their hearts to God. Christianity is our product; it's what we "sell."

The Model: The Local Church

When you go to any church, before you see Jesus, you see the people and how they express their faith in Christ in a local setting. There are distinct brands within the different models—including Baptist or Pentecostal, mainline denomination or charismatic. Some models are program-based, some are liturgical, and other models are small-group-driven or even prophetic. The fact is that there are enormous variations in how Christianity is presented to the world. Still, your local church is a "showroom" for Christianity. The question is, will the visitors "buy"? Will they at least "test-drive"? Or will they leave and never return?

The Dealership: The Building, Music, Staff, and Service

The "dealership" is the combination of the physical plant and campus, the pastor and his staff, the volunteers and the programs that are offered. Within each dealership is a value system that drives the staff to accomplish specific goals. Some want to reach the lost, some want to reach unfulfilled Christians, and some want to enlist more members for financial support. Still others want more people involved to support the personal goals and lifestyle of the pastor. When you research a church, it becomes obvious why the particular "dealership" exists.

The Parts Department: Where People Find What They Need

Many churches omit the parts department, the place where spiritual enhancements are added to your life. This is where you are equipped for ministry or to deal with life issues.

Relationships can begin and grow here. Most often this takes place in small groups that meet in homes, in recreational places, or sometimes at the church itself.

The Service Department: Where People Get Fixed

My wife drives a Hummer H3. She loves it. Recently when she had engine problems she made an appointment with the dealership to have it repaired. Needless to say, when she got there she didn't drive the vehicle onto the showroom floor; she drove around to the service department where people get their vehicles fixed. It would look strange sitting on the showroom floor with the engine all torn apart and grease and oil everywhere. So it is when people's lives are broken and need to get fixed. They go to the church's service department.

Typical ministries within this category might include addiction recovery, marriage counseling, and freedom ministries where people can deal with hurt and pain. These ministries may include the use of spiritual gifts for giving special prophetic messages or words of knowledge and wisdom. In a life-giving church, these ministries would take place in a private place where the dignity of the individual is honored and distractions are minimized. This might be the pastor's office, a counseling room, or a special retreat environment. This needs to be a separate place; after all, a service technician at Rolls-Royce wouldn't rebuild the engine on the showroom floor.

The Showroom Floor: The Worship Service

Here is where the product is displayed for the world to see. There are as many kinds of showrooms as there are models of churches, from traditional to contemporary. In one you might discover a sense of ancient ritual with deep historical roots. In another, present-day themes are emphasized and religious overtures are ignored or purposely avoided. In another, you'll see displays of joy and emotional demonstrations. What people see and experience on the showroom floor will affect their decision of whether or not to buy. Therefore, you have to be very careful with the customer experience on the showroom floor. Some things when they were new drew visitors in mass numbers, but now they don't. Almost every practice has an expiration date.

The Lost Sheep and the Showroom Floor

The showroom floor analogy is perhaps incomplete because of all the nuances that exist in the local church ministry. Still, it helps us focus on providing a safe environment to encourage the under-churched to experience Christianity in a local church setting.

The goal is to reach the lost with the understanding that we as church members may have to give up some familiar Sunday morning traditions. When we provide at least this one service each week for God's lost sheep, we have accomplished more than we would by tailoring the service for our current host of believers. This one hour per week is dedicated to those who don't yet attend.

Consider Luke 15:1–7:

Tax collectors and other notorious sinners often came to listen to Jesus teach. This made the Pharisees and teachers of religious law complain that he was associating with such despicable people—even eating with them! So Jesus used this illustration: "If you had one hundred sheep, and one of them strayed away and was lost in the wilderness, wouldn't you leave the ninety-nine others to go and search for the lost one until you found it? And then you would joyfully carry it home on your shoulders. When you arrived, you would call together your friends and neighbors to rejoice with you because your lost sheep was found. In the same way, heaven will be happier over one lost sinner who returns to God than over ninety-nine others who are righteous and haven't strayed away!" (NLT).

We all know the story of the lost sheep and how the shepherd leaves all the others to find the one. But look at the rationalization. "In the same way, heaven will be happier over one lost sinner who returns to God than over ninety-nine others who are righteous and haven't strayed away!"

This is Jesus talking. He says that He is more interested in reaching the one sinner than He is in maintaining the flock that He has. He even risks losing some of the existing flock, the ninety-nine, by leaving them alone to face possible danger so that He can go find one lost sheep.

Since this is the heart of God to reach the lost, we should be on an unending quest to create an inviting environment for lost sheep in our local churches, small groups, and outreaches, one that will effectively bring them back into the fold. And when the services are filled with those who need Christ, and when they respond to the message of salvation, the current believers will respond with great joy. This joy becomes a huge motivation for church members to bring lost friends to our services.

What's the Big Deal?

The big deal is that if the Sunday morning experience is a turn-off, you may never see those visitors again. Plenty of visitors to local churches don't return after a boring service or inappropriate behavior by members of the congregation.

The showroom floor—the Sunday morning experience—needs to be protected from the agendas of certain individuals and the mis-use of spiritual gifts. Why? It has been my experience that in most churches Sunday morning is when visitors and the "unlearned" attend church. They come unaware of what church is all about, and they require our sensitivity. This may be the only opportunity to reach them for Christ or at least make church a relevant, uplifting experience for them.

So what are the behaviors that spoil a good showroom experience? You've seen them and I've seen them. They are the spoilers that detract from the Sunday morning experience: a never-ending sermon...an increasingly spooky and weird worship set...an offering message that lasts for half of the service...irrelevant announcements that rail on like a never-ending graduation ceremony...hard preaching that condemns and offers no hope.

Another huge turnoff is allowing people to exercise their spiritual gifts at the expense of everyone else. In my personal experience, most of the time this blesses no one and creates more questions than answers. Spiritual gifts should be exercised—but could there be a better place and time to exercise them than Sunday morning service at your church? Is Sunday morning the best place for random people to exercise their vocal gifts? Should we give them full access to the service just because they have a gift? They may come from a dysfunctional church with an agenda; should they be allowed to transfer their dysfunction to your Sunday service? It seems as though people default to previous experiences when they come to a new church. And a few vocal people can hijack your vision if you let them.

It's like changing the oil on the showroom floor. It's not that you don't value oil changes—they're vital aspects of a car's maintenance—it's just that you don't do it on the showroom floor where everyone can see. The same applies to the use of some spiritual gifts. Look at what the apostle Paul says in 1 Corinthians 14:23: "If the whole church comes together and everyone speaks in tongues, and some who do not understand or some unbelievers come in, will they not say that you are out of your mind?" (NIV). Paul is not devaluing the gift of tongues; rather, he is defining the gift's use.

In the same way we must define the use of everything we do. We must decide if a practice belongs on the showroom floor or somewhere else...in a different place, at a different time. And in deciding, our goal must be to never turn away the very guests we are trying to reach. The best rule of thumb to remember is this: The power is constant, but the practice is fluid.

The Deeper Life

Okay, so we have great Sunday services. There are lots of visitors. Christians and non-Christians alike come and feel safe and secure. But what about the rest of what we need from the church experience? When can people experience the deeper life with God? Many churches are accused of being "a mile wide and an inch deep." How then do we deepen our relationships with almighty God?

Sundays alone are not enough to bring members into the deeper truth and life of God. Let's face it, one hour a week is not going to bring much change to a person's life. It can have an impact, but real change comes through discipleship. Sunday is not the only discipleship day. It is the most important day of the week to share the gospel as it relates to the felt needs of the members and visitors alike. To try to make Sunday the day to go deep with believers is to ignore the needs of underchurched guests.

There are six other days that we can devote to intense Bible study, healing services, and the discovery of spiritual gifts. There can be days for recovery ministries, intercessory prayer, small groups, and anything else that brings people into a deeper, more meaningful walk with God. However, if they don't get saved, or if they don't feel comfortable in the Sunday service, you will never have the opportunity to bring them into that closer walk with God.

Simply put, if they are not coming back to Sunday services, all the "deeper life" programs in the world can't help them. Sunday can build up believers but not anything like small groups and personal one-on-one ministry.

It all begins with providing a time where the lost can come and be exposed to the gospel of Christ in an environment that draws them back again. Once this is accomplished and your building is being filled each week with visitors who return again and again, you will discover that many will give their hearts to Christ and you will be able to lead these new converts into the deeper life with God.

Pastor Chris Hodges at Church of the Highlands in Birmingham, Alabama, has successfully built this model of church. With thousands receiving Christ on Sundays, the Wednesday night services are packed with believers who want more teaching and more time to respond to God on a personal level. On one particular Wednesday night, more than two hundred new believers had a unique encounter with the Holy Spirit. At a men's retreat, more than six hundred had the same deep experience with the Holy Spirit. This didn't happen on Sunday while the underchurched guests were being reached, but on another evening of the week designed especially for the deeper life experience. On Sundays, Pastor Chris starts with strong Bible-based messages and then offers opportunities for his congregants to find more in a variety of venues.

The Power Is in the Seed, and the Seed Is the Word

Everything we do must begin and end with the Word of God. There is no other source for truth about God and salvation outside of the Word. We must never neglect the preaching of the Word, even for the sake of "getting people to come." What are they coming for? They are coming for life-transforming truth that can be found only in the Bible. In every "showroom" presentation of Christ in the local church, the Word must be preached in the fullness that it is revealed in Scripture. Make sure, however, that it is God's Word you preach and not your opinion. Preaching with grace and power will bring forth fruit when the environment is right.

Too often, pastors preach some new interpretation or revelation that is nothing but fluff. It is a distraction that keeps them occupied, and it leads the people astray. It is not the Word, but rather the private interpretation of Scripture.

The Word of God must be the basis for reaching the underchurched world and for making disciples of Jesus. Once the underchurched buy into the showroom floor experience, all the other discipleship efforts will become exciting and fulfilling. Try it and see how soon your auditorium begins to buzz with the sound of seekers finding true riches in Jesus Christ.

Chapter Four

First Impressions in the Soybean Field

Some years ago, I met an incredible young pastor from Clayton, North Carolina. He and his wife and their three children live in a small farming community outside Raleigh. Matt and Martha Fry work together at Cleveland Community Church, which they started together a few years before. The church is vibrant and growing and now has more than three thousand in attendance on Sundays.

From the time you drive onto the church property until the time you pull away, you are positively impressed with the people, the worship, the message of the pastor, and the entire ministry. It is an amazing church in the middle of a soybean field, and it reaches thousands of people in that area. How did it happen? It all started with the right first impressions. In his own words, Matt explains what they did to build Cleveland Community Church, known today as C3.

Matt's Story

A first impression can never be taken away. When you walk into a restaurant and the floor is sticky, the tables are dirty, and the food is terrible, do you rush out to tell your friends to try the new restaurant? Of course not! On the other hand, if you see a great movie or discover a wonderful new restaurant, you want to invite friends so they can enjoy the same experience. Why should church be any different? Our level of customer service in the church should be far beyond what we can experience at any movie theater or restaurant or store.

When my wife, Martha, and I were called to start a church, we weren't exactly sure where God would take us; we only knew that we would go. After much prayer and guidance, God brought us to Clayton, North Carolina, and we were asked to pastor a new church plant that was meeting in a local elementary school.

Our first Sunday, we walked into the cafeteria where the church was meeting and it looked like just that, a cafeteria. There were murals of animals painted on the walls and elementary school paraphernalia everywhere. My first thought was that this didn't feel like a church. The room was stark and there were only about twenty-five chairs set up in front of the small stage. The cafeteria tables were still standing and simply pushed aside. No effort had been made to create a welcoming environment.

I thought, *How can this be? God has called us here, and the vision He gave me was so big.*

I immediately expressed my concerns and took action to have the tables taken down and more chairs set out. We needed to prepare for the people God would bring through our doors. Well, as you can imagine, being the new kid on the block, I faced a little resistance. After some vision casting, and the fact I began moving the tables myself, the team jumped on board. Before you knew it, the elementary cafeteria began to look and feel more like the church I had envisioned.

From that point on, the team began arriving early. Tables were put away and replaced each weekend. More chairs were set up, along with welcome tables. Coffee was served, and our guests were ushered to their seats. Every effort was made to help members and visitors feel cared about and accepted. We wanted the people to come as they were, and they did. As people responded, our small church plant grew to hundreds. Putting forth a little extra effort in what we were doing was making a kingdom impact.

Our church, C3, continued to grow, and we were later blessed with land so that we could build our first building. We carried these values of a small personal church into our new, much larger facility.

Authors Tony Morgan and Tim Stevens explain that the primary purpose of the church should be to love others: "Remember, it's not about us. It's about the people we're trying to reach for Jesus. It's about the people we're trying to help take their next steps toward Christ. It's about helping the hurting and the hopeless. It's about being Jesus to the community around us."[1]

When I preach, I want to hit a home run every time, connecting with hearts to change people's lives. But long before the service starts, we have an opportunity to connect people to God. The sermon really begins long before guests drive onto the campus for the first time. We communicate to them that we care in the ways that we prepare.

Back in November 2001, I preached a sermon on how important it is for the church family to be prepared to receive and respond to that hopeless person who might walk through the door, perhaps to give God one last chance. After that service, Rob and Karen came to me to share their story. Their family moved here from Ohio that August and immediately began looking for a church home. When the 9/11 terrorist attacks happened, Karen fell apart. She shared how the Sunday after the attacks they went to a small local church, hoping for comfort and answers—but no one cared. For that church, it was business as usual, even though she was a mess. After weeks of uncaring church experiences, she eventually began doubting God's existence because she couldn't seem to find Him.

Karen gave up looking, but Rob did not. Just a week before this particular weekend of services, Karen told her husband, "I'll go to church with you next Sunday, but you better pick a good one, because it's your last chance." Rob chose C3 Church.

Karen didn't expect much, certainly not the love our road signs seemed to promise. She and Rob shared how they were greeted and directed to their kids' classes. Karen recalled how overwhelmed she felt just to walk down the hall to a preschool class. But Dona, who served at the welcome table that day, told her simply, "Let me take you there," and she put her arm around Karen's shoulders to guide her. Dona asked where the family had moved from, what they liked to do, and where they were living. She shared names of C3 members who had similar interests and backgrounds. She touched Karen's heart.

Rob and Karen shared how their son's shyness had led to bad experiences at other churches and how unaccommodating those churches had been. Karen then told me what her son's teacher at our church had done. He had dropped down on one knee and with a warm smile asked, "Buddy, do you see all the girls in this room? I really need a man to help me out." Her son waltzed right in and never looked back.

In those first months, the only ministry Karen could offer was folding worship programs; she had so much healing to do. As her heart healed, she moved through our children's ministry department, from small-group leader to leading our children's discipleship program. She created new ministry teams in our First Touch ministry, and then led the entire First Touch team. Now, she is a leader of leaders in our church, raising up others to reach out to the lost and hurting. She also oversees our community service projects, extending Jesus' love beyond our doors.

And it all began when one lady chose to be the hands and feet of Jesus, when she went the extra mile when Karen was too broken to walk down a hall by herself.

The Media: A Church's Friend

As I mentioned, God brought us to Clayton, but He did not bring the masses with us, if you know what I mean. There is no mall, not even a grocery store nearby. In the early days, my office was thirty minutes away from the church site in a refurbished barn. For this reason, I intentionally reached out to the local newspaper editors and journalists. There was no hidden agenda or request; I just wanted to connect with the community. By taking time to get to know them as individuals and showing them that we cared, we were blessed with free publicity in local papers, and, most recently, a prime-time story on the local newscast.

We learned early on that technology and media are useful tools in building the kingdom in today's society. We currently reach out through our website, podcasts, and my blog. In his book *Beyond the First Visit*, church consultant Gary L. McIntosh explains that the

World Wide Web is the way of life for millions of people. The corporate world has figured out how to tap into it, to understand that with the Internet, businesses are only a click away from an audience of millions. They embrace that opportunity. Forward-thinking church leaders should understand that this opportunity exists for them too.[2]

C3 has seen firsthand the impact the Internet has on people. We've heard from people across the country and overseas who are connected to us through our website and podcasts.

One family shared how God touched their lives through a Sunday message, and that God had actually been using C3 to work in their lives for weeks before they arrived. When they moved to the Raleigh area and began searching for a church home, they did it the modern way, by googling churches on the Internet. They came across our church website and heard several sermons on podcast. They are glad we made church available to them that way, because they felt comfortable and connected before they ever had a chance to set foot on our campus.

It took me a while to warm up to blogging because I've never been very good at keeping a daily journal or diary; I'm a man of few words. But our younger, tech-savvy staff kept working on me and finally convinced me to join the blogging world. Author Brian Bailey explains the effectiveness of blogging in the church:

> Christianity is about others. The local church is about others. If others are not the focus of everything we do in the church, we might as well pack up our bags and go home. When we turn inward, we are literally turning our back on our community. That includes blogging. There is no blogging revolution without others. There is no return on ministry without others. The heart of a blogging church is passionate pursuit of people who matter to God. Blogging is an incredible way to start conversations, reach out to others, develop relationships and build community.[3]

In its first fifteen months, my pastor's blog received more than fifty-eight thousand hits, with an average of a hundred each day. I've shared my joys and hurts, gotten into debates about barbecue and NASCAR, and connected with kids, adults, and friends far away. Blogging really is a great tool to connect with the community around us.

Signs and Parking: Drawing People into Church

In the early years, when we were meeting in a school, road signs were essential in directing people to our church. We strategically placed large signs at major intersections so people would know about us.

One of our longtime members, Paul, found us because of those signs. Paul and his wife had recently moved to the area and were church shopping. Well, actually his wife was church shopping and Paul was busy thinking of every excuse he could not to attend. He suggested C3 to his wife because he was sure she would refuse to go to a church that met in a school. But she agreed, and he honored his word and accompanied her to our church.

Through the years, Paul and I have recalled many times how that first impacted his life. He had never met such genuine, caring people. While attending C3, he was touched by the greeting, the hospitality, and the concern people had for him and his wife. He watched the way people served.

In those days, when we had only about two hundred people including children, everyone—including the senior pastor—pitched in to do everything. We set up the cafeteria, the kids' areas, and the atrium hospitality area. Then some people greeted, while others taught, ushered, and served. Everyone had a "whatever it takes" attitude that really spoke to Paul. Within just a couple of weeks, he and his wife were plugged into church. They were baptized and have been servant leaders here ever since.

Even though we are in our own building now, we still put out fifteen to twenty small signs each weekend at intersections to guide people to church. We recently added an interstate billboard inviting people to join us. The effort, time, and money invested in signs are well worth it when a lost or hurting person says, "I came because of the sign."

But it's not enough to get people here. As Paul's story shows, that's when the chance to care really begins. Author Dale Galloway shares that the way to make sure your first-time guests have a great first experience is "to see things through their eyes."[4] Consider what you do as a church and whether you're sending a message of acceptance and welcome. What are you doing to tell your guests that they matter?

One way our volunteers show they care is by saving the great parking spots close to the building for our guests. When I arrive on campus for weekend services, all the staff members and volunteers' cars are parked out on the "back forty." The prime spots in our paved lot close to the building are wide open and waiting for our guests.

When we moved into our own building, we created a parking team. We weren't so large a church yet that we needed one for safety; we did it to serve our guests with excellence. A motivated parking team accomplishes that. Author Gary L. McIntosh explains that parking teams serve a greater purpose than just guiding people to parking places:

> For most guests, getting out of their car and walking up to the church building is a major moment of truth. Some start to feel tense as they imagine what they will find inside the church building. Will there be warm and friendly people? Are they entering the building by the proper door? Will they need to ask a lot of embarrassing questions? Are they dressed appropriately?[5]

The friendly smiles and directions offered from the parking team members offer security and acceptance before people ever approach the building.

One of our parking team members has served faithfully on the team for several years. He has been asked to join other teams, but he won't. He explains that when he first came to C3, the parking team made him feel welcomed in a way he had never experienced at church before. He wants to be sure that whenever he can, he offers that same comfortable welcome to our guests. He serves rain or shine, and at special events throughout the week. This guy understands the true purpose of the parking team and he lives it out each week.

The Welcome Teams: The Caring Continues

The welcoming atmosphere set in the parking lot has to continue into the building. Gary L. McIntosh states that "most guests will make a judgment about your church within thirty seconds of entering the front door." Guests today do not want to be singled out. Yet they want people to acknowledge that they exist, that they are real people. They want to know there is hope and that God has a plan for them.[6]

One of our volunteers recognized an opportunity to reach out when a teenage girl came to church with her dad. She obviously wasn't happy about being at church. She wouldn't make eye contact with anyone. This volunteer said hello to her and got no response. The volunteer shared how she silently prayed for God to touch that girl's life during the service. After service, that same teenager was smiling and talking to people. This time, the volunteer had a chance to talk with her and gave her a compliment. This teenager was blessed because she had not been judged.

One thing that stands out in this volunteer's story is how she welcomed that teenage girl. She was sensitive to the girl's needs and approached her accordingly. That teenager was closed off when she arrived at church, and a hug probably would have shut her down completely. This volunteer understood and stayed back, offered a hello and a prayer, and let the Holy Spirit do His work instead. After service, the volunteer took the time to reach out when she had the opportunity; she sought out this smiling girl to compliment her. She loved this girl just as Jesus would demonstrate His love. And you never know whose life may be changed for eternity because you were there to extend God's love to them.

People know if our welcome is genuine or not. We can smile and welcome them and still be totally insincere. Or, like this volunteer, we can love with the heart of Jesus. Everyone wants to feel accepted and appreciated. Kirk Nowery explains that when we communicate genuine acceptance, others feel affirmed, Christian and non-Christian alike. We should live in a manner that is loving and full of grace. Our behavior influences whether other people are drawn to Jesus or are pushed away from Him.[7]

The Ushers: Smiles in the Aisles

Ushers have the same opportunity to build relationships as other volunteers do. One woman who was a member of our church for many years had a nerve problem in her legs. When she first started attending, no one knew of her physical struggle. In time, she came to know people on our welcome teams and admitted her difficulty standing and sitting. They passed her problem along to the ushers, who took it upon themselves to help her.

A chair with arms would help her to stand and sit and enjoy the full worship experience at church. The ushers tracked down an office chair with arms and moved it into our worship center. They got to know her family and prepared a place for them each week before they even arrived. When her family missed a week, the entire team noticed and cared. The usher team had developed an authentic relationship with this family and was willing to go the extra mile to meet their needs.

The ushers play a large role in our church experience, welcoming and seating our guests and members, passing out worship programs, collecting the tithes and offerings, and participating in special elements during services. Yet, when they take the time to care for people like this lady, they are truly serving as the hands and feet of Jesus, meeting people's needs so they can receive the love of God. As Dale Galloway says, "Almost nothing is more important to visitor retention than to have smiling, friendly, helpful ushers. Train them to remember that first impressions are lasting impressions."[8]

Transformed Hearts: Kingdom Impact

Excellent restaurants have learned the secret of success: great customer service that focuses on the details, including the atmosphere, the quality of the food, cleanliness, and attention to detail. In such restaurants, the customers' wants are more important than the menu. Relationship building and excellence lead to repeat visits, a win for the customer and a win for the restaurant.

Successful businesses understand marketing and the importance of reaching out to people where they are. They keep up with events in the world, and they adapt as needed to reach their target customers.

We can accomplish these same things in the church and make a far greater impact—that is, eternal life in Christ. Jesus has commanded us to "go and make disciples of all nations" (Matt. 28:19 NIV). He didn't ask us to wait for people to come in and conform to our church's way of doing things.

By applying consistent principles that focus on our guests, churches can make a potentially life-changing first impression by:

- Dedicating themselves to do whatever it takes to make sure their guests feel welcome each weekend.
- Loving guests as Jesus would, meeting them where they are instead of asking them to come to us and our way of thinking.
- Being real, investing in authentic relationships that are built on genuine care and acceptance.

Of course, Jesus said it best: "A new command I give you: Love one another. As I have loved you, so you must love one another. By this all men will know that you are my disciples, if you love one another" (John 13:34–35 NIV). No customer will ever forget that kind of care; no customer will want to live without it.

PART TWO

The Experience of the Attractional Church

Chapter Five

Environmentally Friendly Evangelism

I once was asked to speak at a conference in Tennessee that was attended by several hundred pastors whose churches were struggling and somewhat ineffective. These great men and women had paid a huge price to preach Christ and the power of a Holy Spirit–led life.

As the first speaker, I tried to make the case for preaching a relevant message on Sunday that people could connect with on Monday. I shared the need for creating an environment that the underchurched would find safe and enjoyable so they would receive the message of Christ.

I said that Christ never changes, but the methods we employ must change to relate to every person in the pew. In other words, the message must pass the "Who cares?" test. I tried to help the attendees see that the content of the message *plus* the way it's delivered will impact and bring positive change into the hearers' lives.

The other conference speaker was a well-known and faithful man who had written many books and has lots of national influence among similar church groups. With good intentions, he contradicted much of what I said by exclaiming to me and the entire group, "Billy, you don't have to be relevant, just preach the Word! If you just preach the Word, it'll do the rest."

I failed to get my message across. Very few embraced it; after all, who can argue with "preaching the Word"? But I see three inherent problems with this pastor's comments.

First, I assumed that every pastor in the place taught the Bible. I don't think they preached out of newspapers or from what they learned at the movies, so "preaching the Word" was not the issue.

Second, since the pastors all preached the Bible but were still seeing no growth, the pastor's comment reinforced the lack of relevance in their *method*.

Third, if preaching the Word would do it, why wasn't it getting done? It couldn't be the fault of the Word or the message, so it must be the fault of the method.

If God's Word was powerful all by itself, why would we even need preachers? We'd simply stand up and read the Bible publicly with no commentary whatsoever. But when Ezra read God's Word publicly, the Bible says explicitly that he made it "clear," and gave the meaning "so that the people could understand what was being read" (Neh. 8:8 NIV). Acts 14:1 says that Paul and Barnabas "spoke so effectively that a great number of Jews and Gentiles believed" (NIV). This means that it's not enough to merely preach God's Word.

The precedent set by our biblical heroes demands that we too communicate God's Word *effectively* and *clearly*. In other words, relevance is a biblical mandate, not a worldly pursuit.

The Parable of the Sower and the Seed

In the parable of the sower and the seed in Matthew 13:1–23, Jesus presents the results of seeds sown in different environments—different types of soil.

Some soil was not conducive to growth and so the seed was either stolen away, produced little fruit, or didn't germinate and grow at all. In other words, the Word could not produce fruit in the wrong environment! It sounds close to heresy to say that God's Word needs the right environment to be effective, but according to the parable, this is the case.

The environment in this parable is the hearts of the hearers. Some people do not understand the Word, so the evil one steals what was planted in their hearts. Then there are others who hear the Word and at once accept it with joy—but since they have no root, their belief withers. When trouble or persecution comes because of the Word, they quickly fall away. Next are the ones who receive the seed that falls among the thorns. These are people who hear the Word, "but the worries of this life and the deceitfulness of wealth choke it, making it unfruitful" (Matt. 13:13–22 NIV).

Finally, we come to the people whose hearts are ready to receive the Word. "The one who received the seed that fell on good soil is the man who hears the Word and understands it. He produces a crop, yielding a hundred, sixty or thirty times what was sown" (Matt. 13:23 NIV).

What I learn from this parable is that God's Word is all-powerful and able to produce fruit in a person's life. But if the heart is not prepared to receive it, it can bear little or no fruit at all. The failure is not the fault of God's Word but the state of the heart. And so, what can we do to prepare people's hearts to receive God's Word—to be the good soil for this seed?

Our challenge is to create an environment in our churches that prepares the hearts of hearers to receive the Word, so they in turn will bring forth much fruit. Is it possible that we can "prepare the soil" of the hearts of hearers to be more receptive? Is there one environment where the Word of God is more readily understood and received? Yes, I believe there is…and many attractional churches around the United States have found ways to create that fruitful environment.

Relevant Connection

Like it or not, you are leading a church in the twenty-first century. You are preaching and teaching in the era of niche marketing, mobile news, Wikipedia, and made-to-order fast food. This is the iPhone generation. People today are Tweeting, Facebooking, Tok-Boxing, and Skyping. Who knows what they'll be doing tomorrow? One thing is certain: People are accustomed to getting the information when and where they need it. Information is king.

This is why we can't simply preach the Word in the same ole way. There's no doubt that the Word of God is our daily bread and the light that guides our path, but it is effective only when it is delivered in a way that is understood and internalized. That's precisely why Jesus used everyday objects and examples that were relevant to His day. The truth is, we are not very familiar with mustard trees in America, leprosy is all but cured, and no one runs around naked in graveyards breaking chains like the demon-possessed man of Gadara.

I believe that if Jesus were preaching today, He'd be talking about the mortgage crisis, the health-care debate, and the prevalence of online pornography. Why? Because people connect with us when we address their real, felt needs. They don't connect with religious lingo that they can't understand. Let me be clear that the Bible is the absolute authority and is 100 percent true. But we have the responsibility to translate the truth into illustrations that reflect today's realities.

Greg Surratt, senior pastor of Seacoast Church in Mount Pleasant, South Carolina, and one of the founding members of the ARC, is a great example of relevant connection. Every Sunday he prepares his message with two people in mind, the visitor and the believer. He often says that it takes twice as long to prepare a message that has something for everyone as it does to prepare for just the visitor or just the lifelong Christian.

Instead, Greg does what Robert Morris, lead pastor of Gateway Church in Southlake, Texas, calls having a "shallow end and a deep end" in every talk. Greg's goal is not to say something profound, but to say something relevant that has profound results. After attending Seacoast Church for several years, I can tell you that Greg's messages contain deep truth to challenge the seasoned believer, but this truth is packaged in such a way that visitors feel connected. They walk away with something practical they can apply that very week.

The most effective pastors today are not only preaching God's Word in its tried-and-true historical text; they are making it come alive to this present generation. They are preaching the truths of the Word of God in ways that are engaging and compelling. The most effective pastors develop sermon series that address the relevant issues of our time.

Making the Word Twenty-First Century Relevant

Here are some key points on how to share the Bible in a relevant way.

Relate a Biblical Story to Real Life Today

It may be hard to relate a verse about "wheat and tares" or a demoniac living in a cemetery to contemporary situations, but the story is in there. We all have resistance from the enemy in preaching God's Word, and we have to deal with it. Whatever the Scripture, read it until it speaks to something in your own life. Then put it into modern language. Here are some ways to do that:

Create, then solve a problem. The problem could be lack of finances, illness, relational issues, or something else. Use the Scripture to highlight the problem, then make it personal.

Tell where you or someone you know has failed or struggled in a similar situation. We all go through the same trials and struggles, some more intense than others, and the listeners want to hear how you dealt with your issues. Be transparent, but not overly transparent. They don't need to hear about all your dirty laundry.

Show them practical ways you found solutions. Once you have identified the problem and shared how you dealt with it, give your listeners several practical steps for solving their own problems. Make the steps obvious, easy, and strategic. For example, if the problem is poor communication in the marriage, teach them first how to listen, next how to talk to one another without getting offensive, then how to initiate conversations in a positive way.

Give them steps to avoid going there again. Give them principles they can live by to avoid making the same mistake in the future. For example, if the issue is financial debt, show them how to retire the debt, live within their means, and be generous.

Share a Biblical Truth

Truth is what the Bible is all about. Share a fact in the Scripture and apply it to everyday life.

Tell About Misunderstandings of the Truth

This is where you help people who have tried to use that truth in their personal lives but were unsuccessful. Maybe they don't understand it the way it is written. For example: "Forgive, and you will be forgiven" (Luke 6:37 NIV). This does not mean that others will have to forgive you before you forgive them. It means that you must forgive others before God will forgive you!

Give a Strong Biblical Basis for the Truth

This is where a short Bible study will reinforce what the other Scriptures have said.

Show People How to Apply the Truth to Their Lives

Here is where you get practical. Give your listeners steps for implementing and applying the truth to everyday life situations.

Grade Your Message

Listen to your message and ask yourself, *Did I create a path whereby God could connect with the real-life situations of my listeners? Did the lights go on? Was I creative or contemporary?* The measurement is connection. If the lights of understanding came on for someone so he or she knows how to apply the text to real life, you have succeeded.

Again, your church can be relevant and life-giving. You are the key. If you take the time to tailor your messages to the real needs of your listeners, they will be changed forever—and you will have created an attractional church.

For a sampling of the series that some attractional churches are preaching, just browse through the websites of the churches represented by the ARC lead team at www.arcchurches.com.

Chapter Six

The Power of Relationships

Some places have it and some places don't.

Have you ever visited a church, and as you walked out to your car and began to drive away, you felt an overwhelming sense that you had just experienced something special? That you did more than just visit but truly belonged there, as if you were *home*?

Most of us have experienced churches and organizations like this: places that ooze a sense of family and unity and inclusiveness. You feel something different when you are in these places.

That something is the *power of relationships*.

Relationships are the glue that attracts people to our churches and relationships are what keeps them there. Over the years, I've traveled hundreds of thousands of miles and visited hundreds of churches. Usually, I can tell within fifteen minutes if the church has the power of relationships or if it's running on fumes, using the old tricks of finesse and manipulation to keep people coming back.

Signs of Emotional Connection

One of my dearest friends, Rick Bezet, pastors New Life Church in Little Rock, Arkansas. Rick planted one of the first attractional churches in February 2001, and today more than seven thousand people worship together at two campuses. This church exemplifies the power of *emotional connection*.

Here are some ways to create the connection that keeps people coming back.

Be Genuinely Friendly

The first thing you notice at New Life Church is that everyone is *friendly*. Not the kind of friendly where you feel forced to wear a smile and repeat an empty phrase or a rehearsed line, but the kind you get when you put old friends together in a room. There is a genuine sense that the people who go to New Life actually care about you and your family and what's happening in your life.

From the time you enter the parking lot, you are greeted with smiling faces. And that's not just on perfect spring days; that's rain or shine, summer or winter. Once you walk through the doors, you're greeted again, but not in the used-car salesman way. The environment is nonthreatening. No one forces you to sit in a special section or puts a sticker on your shirt or makes you feel like a stranger. Rather, you feel as though you've always belonged in this place, with these people.

And that atmosphere pervades every corner of New Life. The people behind the coffee counter are smiling. The workers in the children's area actually seem happy to see you and your crying kids. The ushers aren't pushy or sour but instead remind you of your favorite uncle.

Even the regular, average church members are friendly. People shake your hand, stop to talk to you, and then—get this—they actually listen when you respond. The whole place pulses with love. Every time I go to New Life, I imagine life as a member of that first congregation in Acts 2:42. It's no surprise that New Life's slogan is "Loving God, Loving People, Loving Life." Yep, that's them.

This emotional connection begins in the heart of the senior pastor, Rick Bezet, for as the senior leader goes, so goes the congregation. You'll rarely, if ever, find a friendly church where the senior pastor is unfriendly. Conversely, where there is a genuinely friendly pastor like Rick, the people of the church reflect the attitude of Christ in him.

This is reinforced not only in the pulpit but in his personal life. Rick doesn't just smile when he preaches; he also practices what he preaches. You'll often find him talking with church members long after services are over, visiting lonely people, and taking advantage of small moments to demonstrate true friendship. I can tell you from personal experience that as long as I have known Rick, he has always been there as a true friend, during good times and bad. He does this not because of his position or mine, but because he follows the example of the truest friend of all, Jesus Christ.

Do Everything with Excellence

Emotional connection is reinforced when things are done with *excellence*. When you walk into a stranger's house or step into a person's car and things are a mess, you feel uncomfortable. In the same way, when our buildings are sloppy, children's spaces are confusing, or the senior leader appears disheveled and unprepared, people feel uncomfortable. But when the music is in tune, the chairs are neatly arranged, and the restrooms are spic and span, excellence is conveyed—and that translates into comfort for members and visitors.

One more thing: Excellence means starting on time. You may think that starting late is just "part of being a family," but I guarantee that when you start late, people sense that you don't value their commitment to God or their sacrifice of several hours of their day. Starting late also reinforces others' habit of showing up late, which begins the endless cycle of later and later start times. Don't do this. Start on time this Sunday and make it a practice every week.

Intimate Friendships

Peter Haas is smart. As a matter of fact, he has to be one of the most intelligent men I have ever met. He and his wife, Carolyn, founded Substance Church in Minneapolis, Minnesota, in 2005, and explosive growth has yielded more than two thousand people in weekly attendance.

When I first met Peter and Carolyn, I wanted to be a part of their lives. They were pastors of Believers Church in Marshfield, Wisconsin, and had a vision for planting a life-giving church in the

Minneapolis area. They were excited about the possibilities before them, and I never doubted that those possibilities would become realities. In just a few years, with Peter's rock-star persona and their intense desire to reach the underchurched, Peter and Carolyn built the foundation for what I believe will become a powerful megachurch in the next five years.

Peter covers all the bases with life-giving weekend services that reach the underchurched and with powerfully relational small groups throughout the community. Here are Peter's thoughts on the value of connection in a local church:

Peter Haas on Connection

The most comprehensive studies are showing that the number one cause of happiness within a local church is not great preaching, great facilities, great programs, or great theology. It is instead something ridiculously simple: the ability to make close friends (*Friendship: Creating a Culture of Connectivity in Your Church* © 2005 Group Publishing, Inc.)

Recently I was talking to a guy who attended a church that was virtually dead. He railed on forever about the mediocre worship and preaching. Their board was deadlocked over silly issues. Their outreach was nonexistent. So finally I asked him, "Why in the world are you still going there?" After a long pause, he said: "Well, two of my best Christian friends go there. And the thought of seeing them every Sunday is just enough to keep me coming back."

At first I was a bit astounded by his answer, but by the end of the conversation, I had to agree with him: Close Christian friends are among the greatest assets that a church has to offer. When I think back on the most satisfying moments of my life, they all occurred when I was surrounded by my best friends—when we vacationed together, ministered together, cried together, and raised our kids together.

For example, I don't remember the lessons in many Bible studies, but I definitely remember when one of our Bible studies turned into a bizarre and macho woodchopping contest in my friend's backyard. And after gut-laughing for about a half hour, watching each other attempt idiotic feats of manly strength, we all poured our hearts out to one another around a campfire. There was intimacy, camaraderie, and adventure (like when the ax slipped out of one guy's hands).

Our fondest memories usually have an unspoken relationship factor that made the experiences fulfilling. So when I began studying the statistical causes of "true church satisfaction," it didn't surprise me to find friendships at the top of the charts.

In fact, Group Publishing commissioned the Gallup organization to study how churches can best "attract and keep people." Of course, there were many interesting answers. But one simple factor thundered above all the rest: Provide every member with intimate friends.[1]

Frankly, when I first read this, I was irritated. I had spent years of my life trying to perfect the ultimate church service. From the worship to the multimedia to the sermon, I've completely devoted myself to Sunday mornings, obsessing over the details in hopes that people would return. For example, our church may have the best multimedia presentation in the whole city, but if we are miserable at connecting people to their new best friends, then we will utterly lose the battle of creating church satisfaction.

And the statistical evidence speaks for itself. According to the Gallup study, if your best friend attends your church, you have a 98 percent chance of being satisfied with your church.[2] In other words, if we can generate amazing friendships for every person who walks through our doors, then we will be 98 percent of the way toward providing them with a satisfying church experience!

The study also found: "[Those] who have church-based friendships that extend outside the weekly worship services—either in small groups, through informal gatherings, or other settings—report exceptionally high levels of satisfaction." In fact, people who had a high number of intimate friends noted significantly higher levels of "spiritual transformation" as well as more "firsthand encounters" with God![3] And if this is true, then friendships could very well be the holy grail of a transformational organization.

But none of this should surprise us. After all, we all know from Scriptures that intimate friendships are essential to transformation.

How Do You Connect with the Underchurched?

Ask yourself, *What are we doing strategically to make people feel comfortable and welcome?* Think of it as bridge building. Jesus did it all the time. Whether it was a party with Matthew's friends, a reception at the wedding of a friend, or an unexpected meal with five thousand strangers, Jesus had a unique way of building a bridge and connecting with the people He was called to reach. The point is that you connect *intentionally* in the way that suits *your* God-given gifts and in the way that's needed by *your* community.

Begin to pray that God will show you the connecting tool He has given you. Most likely, it's already an obvious part of your personality. Let God use it to bridge the gap between the underchurched in your community and the life-giving community of your church.

Once you've discovered the power of connection, you're ready to start working on the weekend experience—so that the connection between people and your church actually sticks.

Relationships That Work

Someone asked one day, "How did you become so successful in all you do?"

The secret to any success I have experienced is that I get along with people for long periods of time. I look at every person I meet as a potential lifelong friend. This usually ends up being a positive experience and adds to the potential of having success.

Following are some tips for creating lasting, satisfying relationships.

Keep Hate and Resentment Out

That means I have to overlook friends' faults, forgive their wrongs toward me, and never let hate enter my heart. Actor Will Smith wrote this verse in his song "Just the Two of Us": "Throughout life people will make you mad, disrespect you, and treat you bad. Let

God deal with the things they do, 'cause hate in your heart will consume you too."[4] Love lasts when the relationship comes first!

Nurturing healthy relationships is vital to growing your church. See to it that your congregation members love one another well.

See Friendship as a Covenant

The key to having successful relationships in any area is to live in obedience to the Word of God. The word *relationship* means to be connected by blood or by marriage. Both of these denote covenants. We are in covenant relationship with the Lord through His blood and we are His bride. We are in covenant relationship with our spouses by marriage. We are in covenant relationship with our families by blood. We are in covenant relationship with the body of Christ through Jesus' blood.

If we look at friendships as covenants, we sense the importance of holding up our end. That is extremely important in marriage. Having been married forty-three years, I notice how faithfully my wife, Charlene, keeps her covenant with me and how I strive to keep mine with her. The same goes with my children and grandchildren. We all have a sense that we are bound to love and serve one another.

Matthew 26:28 says, "This is my blood of the covenant, which is poured out for many for the forgiveness of sins" (NIV). God honored His part of the covenant with humankind by sending Christ into the world to pour out His blood for us. Wow! So what is my part? To faithfully serve Him, honor Him in all I do, and fulfill the mission He gave me in life to accomplish. I have to work at keeping my part of the covenant with God. I admit, it is not always easy!

Make Maintenance a Priority

Relationships take years to cultivate, and if we are not maintaining and growing our relationships, they can be destroyed in a few moments. This means we work on them during the good and the bad times. You learn to like someone when you can laugh together, but you can never know deeper love until you have cried together.

When you share common joy it's great, but when you endure common sorrow together it is wonderful—in the end.

Make Faithfulness and Honesty Your Hallmarks

As I look at friends and loved ones I have had deep relationships with for many years, I realize their faithfulness and honesty mean the most. This is the way we walk in relationship with one another. If we lie or are unfaithful to each other, we don't deserve the relationship. I have noticed that even great men and women carry with them the burden of bad relationships. How much greater their lives could be if those relationships were healed. Most broken relationships are a result of unfaithfulness or dishonesty.

Continuous Fellowship

We need look no further than the early church in Acts 2 to find a perfect example of the power of successful relationships.

Verses 42–47 describe the early believers as having continuous fellowship, eating together, sharing things, and enjoying one other. The Greek term for fellowship here is *koinonia*, which, according to *Strong's Concordance*, means "fellowship, association, community, communion, joint participation."[5] This *koinonia*, or fellowship, is a natural response to finding Jesus: a growing desire to learn more and be a part of the body of Christ.

It is hard to manufacture such fellowship in the local church when no true conversions are taking place. Only when a person is genuinely converted does his new spirit crave such committed fellowship. Inherent in the miracle of the new birth is a hunger for more truth, more of God, and more relationships in the assembly of believers. Christians desire fellowship whenever possible.

Fellowship aids discipleship. The major problem with making disciples is the lack of fellowship. Having a special discipleship class to raise up leaders is not nearly as effective as having continuous fellowship with other believers in the church. Times of fellowship contribute to the best face-to-face discipleship. Discipleship naturally occurs in fellowship. When there is community, communion, caring for one another, and ministry to one another, disciples are made.

On the other hand, if you try to create a discipleship track without fellowship, it becomes difficult. Interaction and fellowship are key ingredients in making disciples. From discipleship come lifestyle evangelism and spiritual growth. Therefore, new disciples are continually added.

That's human relationship at its best: persons coming to a new relationship with Christ.

In conclusion, what makes an attractional church is the dynamic relationships that form among church members. If authentic, life-giving friendships exist in your church, many will be attracted to your doors—and they will stay!

Chapter Seven

Meeting God

For decades, the local church was a picture of what it means to be behind the times in terms of music, video, and the overall worship experience. Not anymore. Many churches today are the premier venues in their cities. Churches have moving lights, billowing fog, movie-theater-quality video, and precisely tuned audio systems. I love the new technology we have in our churches, because I think in many ways it enhances a genuine worship experience. But first and foremost, the worship experience must cultivate the presence of God.

Nothing is more important than bringing people closer to God. In the phases of my own walk with God, I have learned more and more who God is and what it means to genuinely experience Him.

A Personal Encounter with God

My first mental image of God was one with a stern look on His face, His all-powerful arms crossed, waiting for me to mess up so He could punish me. That is what I was told all my life. Mama used to warn, "There is a God in heaven, and when He sees you do something bad, He will punish you."

There were six children in our family, and Mama couldn't do everything for every one of us. So we each had chores like preparing our own breakfast and ironing clothes. One morning when I was around ten years old, I was ironing my shirt. I could just see the top of the ironing board and was pressing a shirt for school. The iron slipped and burned my chest. I screamed and ran to get some ice from the refrigerator. Mama calmly looked at me and said, "See there, God punished you!" If she said this once, she said it hundreds of times. It was her doctrine of God and forgiveness. She wanted to make sure we knew that we were accountable for our actions and the consequences (most likely, punishment) of everything we did.

I never could sense forgiveness from God even though, as an attendee in a local Catholic church, I heard a version of the gospel all my life. Judgment and condemnation were all I remember hearing from preachers in the movies or at other churches. This was my experience, and it was what I had as a basis of faith: Do bad and get punished, but never forgiven. I needed and wanted forgiveness but never seemed to find it.

So this was my God: mad at the world, scornfully looking down with disappointment, and waiting to punish every evildoer...especially me.

Reality of Relationship

As a young man I attended the Louisiana State Police training academy. There I met an atheist. He told me that he was raised a Catholic, had attended a Baptist church for a long time, and had read the Bible. His conclusion: There is no God.

That made me mad. After all, I knew that there was a God in heaven because He had been punishing me all my life, according to Mama. This man's comments were all the motivation I needed to launch a personal research project to prove His existence to an atheist and discover God for myself—the God I always hoped existed.

Years before, I had met a man by the name of Barney Robison. Barney sold me a fence for my backyard when I was twenty-one years old. During this time my wife, Charlene, was battling Hodgkin's disease and was near death. Barney was a Christian and began to pray for our souls. Three years later, I found myself living as Barney's next-door neighbor. Since I didn't own a Bible, I went next door and borrowed his. What a Bible it was. It was one of these huge family Bibles with the Masonic emblem on the front. Since I knew nothing of the Bible, it seemed to be perfect for my research project. I was going to get what I needed to convince the atheist back at the academy that God was real.

Immediately I started studying the Scriptures. I didn't know where to start, so I began in Deuteronomy. There I stumbled upon a passage that opened my eyes to the possibility of having a relationship with God. In Deuteronomy, God tells us, "Behold, I set before you this day a blessing and a curse; a blessing, if ye obey the commandments of the LORD your God, which I command you this day: and a curse, if ye will not obey the commandments of the LORD your God" (11:26–28 KJV).

From life experience, I knew that the second half of this Scripture section was true, but the first half? "A blessing, if ye obey the commandments of the LORD your God, which I command you this day." This was the first time in my life that I saw God as a God of blessing. All I knew before was that I would be cursed!

As soon as that thought sank in, I went into my bedroom, fell to my knees, and asked God to forgive me. I really felt He would. I had asked Him a thousand times before in a religious way, but now it was personal. I wanted a relationship with Him, and I could sense He wanted one with me.

It was through this experience that I began to see God as a loving Savior with His hands reaching out to me. No longer was He mad, waiting for me to mess up. Now He was inviting me to walk with Him. He would be my Lord and my God from that point on.

This great love encounter with God made me realize that I could have a personal relationship with Jesus and that He would give me a deep and sincere love for others…whether they loved me or not.

Certainty of Accessibility

After my conversion, I continued on with the Lord and eventually heard the call to ministry. That was more than thirty years ago.

For many years I lived in the glow of that conversion experience and never looked back. For the most part, I've lived my life on the Mount of Blessings. However, like everyone who lives in this world, I have had disappointments and losses too. Without going into details here, I have lost both parents, a brother, a niece, many close friends, and two grandchildren. My wife has had to deal with cancer since she was twenty-one years old. Time and again, the Lord has pulled her through life-threatening illness, but we have had to live with the emotional and financial toll.

As I look back to the early years of our marriage and the battles we faced without Christ in our lives, I realize that He was always there, reaching down into our situation and lifting us out, even in the midst of spiritual bankruptcy.

For example, in 1971 Charlene was pregnant with our third daughter, Shary, when we found out that she had Hodgkin's disease. She endured surgery and twenty cobalt treatments and suffered intensely. We had to live in a garage apartment for four weeks, and at the end of that round of treatments we were completely broke.

To everyone's surprise, Shary was born healthy. We were not Christians at the time and couldn't conceive how God could do something so wonderful for us. But later we learned we had to go back for more cobalt treatments. This time we had nothing—no money for an apartment and barely enough for food. We took the kids to stay with their grandparents, and off we went.

By God's grace, Charlene's cousin moved to New Orleans and let us stay in their apartment during this six-week period. One challenge, however: There was no furniture for the bedroom we stayed in. We slept on the floor while Charlene continued to suffer severely.

There we were, the woman I loved the most, sicker than she had ever been, and I couldn't even provide a bed or mattress for her to sleep on. What could we possibly have to offer God? *Nothing* is the answer. But God saw value in this helpless young couple. He saw the years that we would serve Him in ministry as pastors, missionaries, and church planters.

Years later, I would read David's account of his service for God. He summarizes his life in 2 Samuel 22:36: "You give me your shield of victory; you stoop down to make me great" (NIV). When we were totally broke, spiritually dead, with no hope in the world, God saw value in us. He stooped down, reached out His hand of mercy, and drew us out of a miry, hopeless pit. He values every human soul.

This gives me the mental picture of God on His knees reaching down into my situation, no matter how low I get. He is accessible even when we cannot imagine that He is there in our desperate moments. But He is there; He is here; He is always present.

Every person who visits our churches wants to encounter God. I always wanted to but never did until my conversion experience. I prayed several times a day—in the morning, before and after meals, and every evening—but I never experienced Him. I believe with all my heart that the reason was my wrong mental image of God. The forbidding, folded-armed God of punishment was detrimental to my experiencing Him.

How Do You Present God?

So the question arises: What image of God do you communicate in your church services? Is it the unforgiving God? Or is it the open-armed God who forever reaches into this human experience and offers His mercy and grace? This makes a huge difference in whether people will encounter God when they come to your church.

The attractional church's offering the presence of God is paramount to the conversion of souls to Christ. Churches that encourage a personal encounter with God become the most vibrant and best represent the body of Christ to their communities.

Stovall Weems, senior pastor of Celebration Church in Jacksonville, Florida, is a perfect example of this. Stovall is a former LSU Tiger who felt the call of God to plant a church in the heart of sun country, the state of Florida.

After just a few years, Celebration Church has been named among the fastest-growing churches in America in *Outreach Magazine's* 2005 issue.[1] Once you've spent a weekend there, you'll know why. Services at Celebration are exactly that—a celebration. Step into Stovall's church on any given weekend and you'll experience worship that is vibrant and full of diversity in both style and ethnicity.

The Sunday experience at Celebration provides a perfect environment for the lost to find forgiveness, for the absent to reengage in a vibrant relationship with Christ, and for the unfulfilled to plunge into the presence of God with a certainty that He is not only there, but ready and willing to respond.

Stovall was determined to create an experience for people that brings them to the line of faith and also shows them what it's like to have a deeply meaningful and rich relationship with the living God. When your church provides these divine encounters, people will leave your building not only in a deeper relationship with God, but eager to lead others to the same.

Avoiding Excess

In Exodus 16 we read the story about God's daily provision of food to Israel. He sent them a daily supply of "manna," the bread of heaven. It was God's response to the Israelites' complaints of not having enough to eat. He gave them this gift with the provision that they limit the amount of manna that each family gathered. Consider Exodus 16:19: "Moses said unto them, 'No one is to keep any of it until morning'" (NIV).

Of course, some didn't listen. Verse 20 reveals what happened: "However, some…kept part of it until morning, but it was full of maggots and began to smell. So Moses was angry with them" (NIV).

What happened here was that the wonderful provision of manna became stinky and full of maggots when gathered and kept in excess! Such a wonderful gift became disgusting rot when used in an excessive way. In the right amount, the manna was the solution to the hunger of the nation of Israel, but in excess it was offensive and worthless.

In the same way, I have often seen the wonderful provision of the Holy Spirit used in the wrong way, in an excessive, hyperemotional way. Spirit-filled worship becomes a problem to the local church instead of the blessing that God intended it to be. One of the most frequent misuses of spiritual gifts is when non-members use their vocal gifts, tongues, or prophecy, in a Sunday service without the permission of the pastor.

Encounters with the Holy Spirit have been the highlight of my Christian experience. I have experienced joy and the thrill of victory every time the Holy Spirit touches my life. Sometimes my reactions have been somber and worshipful; at other times my response has been exuberant with outward expressions of joy. In each case, these were my own reactions to the Holy Spirit and not His *causing* me to act in any particular way.

Internalizing the Reaction Instead of the Person

In the Bible we read about dramatic encounters with God. How do you explain fire dancing on someone's head or crippled bones snapping together? Or burning bushes, mountains of smoke, walls of water, and falling rock? In some texts we find people dancing, singing, falling over dead, and even ripping off their clothes after an experience with God. A genuine encounter with the Holy Spirit cannot be easily explained, categorized, or mimicked. But the thing to be valued is not the reaction to the power of God, but the encounter with God Himself. We must not confuse the spiritual encounter with our own human reaction to the divine.

Encounters with the Holy Spirit should be a part of every believer's life. However, when we promote *our reactions* to His presence as proof of His approval, we take it to excess. Excess lets people misrepresent who the Holy Spirit is, clouding the meaning of biblical encounters with the Holy Spirit and repelling honest seekers who are trying to find God.

When an excessive reaction to the Holy Spirit is internalized, it can become institutionalized in church services. When this happens, we begin to accept these demonstrations as proof of God's presence and shrink in our search for a genuine encounter with God. We lose our sensitivity to the needs of the lost and begin to defend our behavior, no matter how bizarre. Examples of this are demonstrations of shaking, jerking, vocal outbursts, or laughing. These often go ignored by members even though they repel people or keep visitors from coming back.

Every major revival in history has been accompanied with signs and miracles in people's lives. How can mortal man not respond in unusual and strange ways when he encounters the Almighty. There are reports of all kinds of bizarre and unexplainable events that are well documented during these revivals. The question is, "How long do we try to perpetuate these reactions in a local church setting?" I am not trying to disparage the supernatural events that occur in the presence of a sovereign God, just raising the question about institutionalizing them.

The Passion of Christ

The passion of Christ is to reach a lost world, a world that is dying without knowing His saving grace and therefore plunging into eternal separation from Him. While we should, and do, enjoy the presence of the Holy Spirit in our services, His primary work is to convict the world of sin and draw them to the Father. We must avoid doing anything in public services that impedes the work of reconciliation. This is especially true of excessive emotional demonstrations that distract people from hearing and receiving the message of the gospel.

Pastor Rick Bezet has a general rule of thumb for his congregation: "Worship God any way you want to as long as it does not bring attention to yourself." That's a great way to look at it. After all, worship is designed for an audience of One.

In the final analysis, how we present Christ in our services will either draw people closer to God or repel them from Him. You have probably had both experiences, and so have I. Is He an angry God with retribution in His heart toward us? Or is He a loving God offering us a secure relationship with Him through His Son, Jesus? To a world without Christ we should offer a "God experience" on Sunday that is undeniably an authentic encounter with the Great I Am. It all starts with presenting Him as forgiving, welcoming, and accessible.

When people attend your church service and are drawn to God, they will be back, for there is nothing more compelling—or refreshing—than an encounter with the living God.

Chapter Eight

Aftertaste

After traveling to more than fifty countries of the world and tasting every kind of food imaginable, I believe I've found the best food in the world, and I have to admit, it's not from my home state of Louisiana. I experienced my favorite meal in a troubled and faraway country.

Beirut, Lebanon, was a stop-off after a trip with EQUIP to Cairo, Egypt. When I arrived in Beirut with EQUIP's president, John Hull, and other members of the team, we were taken up the side of a mountain to our hotel. The trip revealed the brutality of violence and wars: mortar shells, small-arms fire, and rocket explosions had left their mark in the form of craters in concrete walls all over the city. However, each evening, the setting sun cast a beautiful, luminous glow on the beach and city alike.

In the midst of a battered city that remains in turmoil today, I had my greatest culinary experience. While I can't remember all the details of the multicourse meal, it left a very good taste in my mouth and in my heart. The aftertaste of my time in Beirut, the wonderful friends I made, and the meals we ate lingers fondly in my memory.

Dinner at Your Church

My wife, Charlene, and I have had the opportunity to travel to more than a hundred churches across the United States and around the world. We actually got a "taste" of what the church in America was serving up. In most cases, the aftertaste wasn't very good. There were wonderful churches that we still talk about today with endearing memories, but for the most part, what we found was disappointing. The struggling churches had several characteristics in common:

- The pastors talked down to the congregation. Their speech was demeaning and in some cases rude. They took a holier-than-thou stance and made everyone else feel like horrible heathens. These pastors seemed mad at the world and the congregation.
- The messages were not only rude but legalistic. This undermines the grace of God by insisting on adherence to rules and regulations that were not necessarily biblical, but instead based on personal preferences.
- Services were too long. There were unending announcements, hour-long sermons, and forty-five-minute song services.
- The people were both superspiritual and unfriendly at the same time, which is typical of legalistic churches.
- The superspiritual people often displayed bizarre antics. It seemed that the pastor and his flock equated the move of the Holy Spirit with weird behavior. Shaking, falling out into the aisle, unbridled dancing, and verbal outbursts were the order of the day.

Now, for the record, I believe in the active power of the Holy Spirit. In fact, I think it is an untapped resource in many of our churches and student movements. I also believe that in Acts 2, the Holy Spirit was the undeniable power that birthed the church of Jesus Christ and is absolutely necessary to birth new churches today. But I have also seen the misuse of the spiritual gifts.

One night, the pastor of a small church we were visiting called Charlene to come forward for prayer. As she approached the pastor, a group of "catchers" gathered around. As he began to shove her with his hand on her head, she eased one foot behind herself to stabilize herself, leaned forward into his hand with both legs

firmly positioned under her, and the tug-of-war began. The harder
he pushed to get her "filled," the more she resisted, balancing herself with the foot behind her. Charlene prevailed that night, she
didn't go down—but we both left feeling a little bewildered.

More characteristics of a struggling church:

- There were long altar calls with the pastor pleading with
the people to get right with God. He would threaten the
people, saying, "You could get killed driving home from
this service and bust hell wide open!"
- Often there were messages on the prosperity of the believer
that almost always led to a plea for money. Sometimes
there was an "offering teaching" with a long, drawn-out
"ask." On several occasions, the preacher/pastor would sug-
gest that women give their jewelry "to reach more souls."
- When we were alone with the pastors, they would tell us
about all the needs of the church, in terms of dollars, and
ask that we go around and share that need with everybody
we knew. *Sure, just what I had in mind.*

After visiting some of these churches, the aftertaste on my spiritual palate made me never want to return. These churches pos-
sessed nothing relevant, relational, or refreshing. They can't grow
because members don't like all that is going on; therefore, they feel
uncomfortable inviting friends and other acquaintances. The result
is stagnation. However, if members like everything their church
does, they will invite everybody they know.

The Right Stuff

In the early part of 1999, I received an invitation to teach a seminar
on small groups at Seacoast Christian Community Church in Mount
Pleasant, South Carolina. A church with such a long name had to
have something going for it. So I took my partner, Carl Everett,
and we held the seminar there. What happened next changed my
entire outlook on the local church in the United States.

To be honest, I had lost any hope that the local church would have much impact on our country. A vast majority of churches had either reached a plateau or were in decline. I couldn't see how things could turn around because I had never seen a model that was really working across the landscape of the country. Some great churches were winning souls and growing, but with the size and scale of those ministries, it was nearly impossible to replicate those models in small- and medium-sized towns.

After the seminar that weekend I visited the services at Seacoast. Wow, that was sweet. For the first time outside my own church, I witnessed a service that excited me when I walked into the building, ministered to me during worship, built me up through the message, and left me wanting more when I left. I found what I had been looking for: a church that could be replicated again and again around the United States. Seacoast had the right stuff.

So, what was it that left such a good aftertaste? Let me explain.

First of all, we were greeted by normal, sincere people who seemed to be genuinely glad we were there. They loved God and it seemed they might even love me. The buzz in the place revealed excitement and an eagerness for the service to begin. The building was under construction, but no one seemed to care; the mood was upbeat and anticipation filled the air.

As the worship began you could tell that it was not a concert but rather an offering to the God of heaven. There were no individuals competing for attention; all attention was on God.

When Pastor Greg was giving his talk, I noticed that he was careful to read the parts that he felt were the most important to his message. He came across not as someone who hoped to impress hearers with his oratory skills but as someone who wanted to "say it right" for the sake of those who needed Christ.

At the end of the service, we were asked to bow our heads and to respond to the message by lifting our hands if we had a need for Christ or anything else. No pressure, no begging, no threats. It was refreshing.

As we left there were more than 150 happy people enjoying free coffee and one another's company. People seemed to love everything about church and were motivated to bring friends.

When I left I thought, *This is what I have been looking for. If I have to move here to learn how this is done, I will.* And so we did.

In September 2001, we moved to Mount Pleasant to join the staff at Seacoast and to catch the spirit of this life-giving church that wanted to reach the lost world around it.

Convinced now that there were churches that could be Spirit-led and relevant to an underchurched world, I began to seek the underlying ingredient.

That was simple: The ingredient was love. Not love secretly tucked away so it had to be discovered to be experienced, but love that was acted out in everything Seacoast did.

Many churches emphasize several things that leave a positive aftertaste in the hearts of visitors, but those all begin with the model of ministry that Seacoast fosters. The people there are life-giving, welcoming, accepting, and authentic, from the time a visitor drives up until he or she drives away. From the people in the parking lot to the pastor in the pulpit, it is all real. It is love in action.

They are relevant, relational, and refreshing.

At Bayside Community Church in Sarasota-Bradenton, Florida, Pastor Randy Bezet will often have ice water or free ice-cream sandwiches to refresh the congregation as they leave on a hot summer day. Pastor Chris Hodges at Church of the Highlands in Birmingham, Alabama, offers copies of the day's message on CD to anyone who wants it. A spirit of serving and generosity pervades Healing Place Church in Baton Rouge, Louisiana. Pastor Dino Rizzo makes sure that people always feel loved, encouraged, one step closer to God, and one step closer to the resolution of real-life problems. What's more, they leave wanting to come back for more. They experience the love of Christ in action and it is addicting.

A Positive Church Experience

Once we learn what gives a person a positive church experience and we begin to implement those life-giving practices, we start to reap the benefit of a good reputation. When your church has a reputation for being life-giving and maintains an environment that feels safe for the underchurched, it becomes an attractional church. What I mean is that whenever someone is asked where a good church in town is, your church is the main one that is mentioned.

You begin to receive word-of-mouth advertising from all kinds of sources.

This word-of-mouth advertising can come from out-of-towners who saw your road signs and stopped to visit. Or it could come from a deacon or a member of another local church who visited with their family and loved the service. They won't leave their church because they serve there, but they send people they know to your church because they liked it so much. They help build your church, all because they left with a positive aftertaste of your ministry.

Simply put, when a church is welcoming and friendly and the message is relevant, the visitors' needs are met and they leave with a desire to return. Also, when there is an obvious lack of manipulation to get you to do something, people look to God alone for guidance and they get to feel Him drawing them closer. Then, when there is no pressure to give but rather a spirit of generosity, people know that it is God, not the pastor, at the helm of the ministry.

All of this works in favor of the local church as a place where church members freely invite their friends and those friends come back on their own…bringing their loved ones with them. When this begins to happen, your church will gain momentum and begin to grow. When your church services leave a good aftertaste in the hearts of visitors and members, they will come back again and again.

Paying the Price to Be Different

Some years ago I was talking with a pastor of a Full Gospel church, trying to explain the importance of transitioning to reach the underchurched community. I explained that people without Christ may not understand the emotional demonstrations in church and that leaders and members should be more sensitive to the lost if they were ever to grow. The pastor's response was troubling to me.

He said, "I have paid too much of a price to be Full Gospel to change now." In other words, "If the people of this community can't accept our style of church, then they will have to go somewhere else to find Christ or not find Christ at all."

This is a sad testimony of a pastor blessed with so great a gift as the Holy Spirit's power and presence, only to reject the reason the Spirit was given in the first place—to make us witnesses of Jesus Christ and to reach the underchurched.

Spiritual gifts were given to the church to bring enlightenment, power, and unity to the body of Christ. But when misused and misappropriated, expression of these gifts can lead to division and confusion. The gifts themselves do not cause the problems; it's the *misappropriation* of the gifts. Look at the apostle Paul's rebuke to the Corinthian church:

> I give thanks to my God always on your account for the grace of God bestowed on you in Christ Jesus, that in him you were enriched in every way, with all discourse and all knowledge, as the testimony to Christ was confirmed among you, so that you are not lacking in any spiritual gift as you wait for the revelation of our Lord Jesus Christ. He will keep you firm to the end, irreproachable on the day of our Lord Jesus. God is faithful, and by him you were called to fellowship with his Son, Jesus Christ our Lord. I urge you, brothers, in the name of our Lord Jesus Christ, that all of you agree in what you say, and that there be no divisions among you, but that you be united in the same mind and in the same purpose. For it has been reported to me about you, my brothers, by Chloe's people, that there are rivalries among you (1 Corinthians 1:4–11 NAB).

Here is the local church in the New Testament that was "not lacking in any spiritual gift," but was divided. In 1 Corinthians 3, Paul said they were carnal, babes in Christ, because they fought and were jealous of one another. The Holy Spirit was given to empower us to reach the world for Christ, bring unity to the church members, and meet our daily needs for spiritual nourishment. The misuse of His gifts does just the opposite: It divides and undermines evangelism and discipleship. If we ignore this, we will certainly leave the wrong impression in the minds of the guests that attend our services. Eventually, we will have no guests at all.

Here's the key: Don't let the gift of the Holy Spirit become a onetime occurrence that you get stuck in and never grow from.

Rather, let it be the beginning of a lifetime experience that you will allow to grow and mature you. Let the functionality, not the manifestation, of the gift be your target. Don't focus on the initial evidence of the Holy Spirit in your life but on the lasting evidence of the Holy Spirit.

When we allow the gifts of the Holy Spirit to flourish in the right way, with the balance that God intended, the result will be life and growth for the local church.

So, how will we serve up the gospel of Christ in our local church to leave the best impression on our guests, so they will desire Christianity and Christ? Leaving a positive aftertaste with visitors brings them back again and gives us an opportunity to share Christ more fully as they learn and grow.

When this happens, we find ourselves experiencing the most powerful kind of marketing—something I've already mentioned called *word of mouth*. Word-of-mouth advertising is incredible as long as our people communicate a clear and concise picture of the vision of our church. This is what I call the art of *telling your story*. We'll look at that next.

Chapter Nine

Telling Your Story

One great catalyst to the growth of the church has been, and will always be, the power of a simple story. It is the case with every church in the ARC, and it has been true ever since Jesus assembled a group of ragtag fishermen two thousand years ago.

Peter talked about being an eyewitness of His majesty. John insisted that he be allowed to tell about the things he had seen and heard. Thomas was murdered for telling his story. Paul's powerful conversion story was a catalyst for early church growth. In fact, most of the New Testament is essentially a God-breathed collection of firsthand accounts from the early church.

And it wasn't just the preachers who told stories of God's grace. The woman who encountered Christ at the well evangelized her community. The man who was delivered from a legion of evil spirits became an early church version of John Wesley, preaching around the entire region.

Jesus must have known that few of His followers would have the oration skills of Paul or the convictions of Peter. But everyone in your church can do what the blind man did and proclaim God's grace. The Bible tells us that after Jesus healed the blind man's eyes, the man went around telling everyone he could find. When cornered by the religious people and skeptics and asked about the morality of his being healed on the Sabbath, the blind man simply replied, "Whether he is a sinner or not, I don't know. One thing I do know. I was blind but now I see!" (John 9:25 NIV).

That was it.

And that was enough.

And for the next two millennia, millions of people have encountered Jesus in a life-altering way and then turned around to tell someone else. The crippled man shouted it to his friends. The woman at the well told her village. The demon-possessed man witnessed to an entire region. And it didn't end there.

Historians and theologians tell us that after the Day of Pentecost, the Christian population in Jerusalem swelled from 120 to well over ten thousand.[1] The people in this new group of believers called "the Way" had a lot in common. Luke tells us that they shared their homes, their food, and even their clothes. They also shared their stories.

Considered a cult by the Orthodox Jewish community of the day, Christians of the early church weren't allowed to worship in the synagogue. However, as a consolation, they were permitted to meet in an area around the temple, a place known as Solomon's Porch. Without a sanctuary and no plans for a new building, they gladly accepted the offer, and Solomon's Porch quickly became the meeting place for new believers.[2]

Just imagine it: thousands of passionate, excited new believers crammed together to worship God and tell their stories. Amazingly, many of these Christians were actual eyewitnesses of Jesus' earthly ministry.

Imagine as one after another stood to tell his or her story. The stories were different, but the essence was the same: *I was a mess. I found Jesus. Now my life is forever changed.*

That's the power of a story. Every one of the people in your church has a story. And your church has a story of its own.

What is the story of your church?

What is the story that people tell after they leave your church and go back to their own Solomon's Porch—to the office break room or the coffee shop or the gym? Helping them tell the story of the Cross and the story of your church could help your church become the transformational agent God wants it to be.

The attractional church is one with a story and a leader who knows how to tell it.

How to Paint a Picture

Good stories have characters in action and a beginning, a middle, and an ending. A lot of information can be given in a single picture, so spark your listeners' imaginations by painting pictures with words or by showing actual photographs or videos of real people, places, or things.

It is important that, when sharing your story, the vision of your church, or its ministry, you give more than mere facts. Paint a verbal picture of the future that will energize and engage your listeners.

What Makes a Story Memorable and Motivating?

Great stories establish characters, time, and location. Tell them the problem you want to solve or the challenge you want others to embrace. Doing so creates a sense of urgency and compels people to listen—and eventually to take action.

Great stories paint a picture of the listeners' involvement. Describe what your members' involvement could mean in terms of fulfilling the vision. What are the probable outcomes? Show your audience members how they can bring about change and positive results.

Great stories include news of recent wins. Celebrate your wins and engage the audience in the victories you hope to achieve. Do this with video, drama, and live personal testimonies (that are well rehearsed). Communicate continually, until everyone knows your story.

Great stories capture imagination. Stories succeed because they capture the imagination of large or important audiences. If the story is important to you, it will be important to them.

Great stories are true. Your vision may not be realized today, but it is true in your heart and you communicate it as a certainty. But stay consistent; audiences are good at sniffing out discrepancies.

Great stories make a promise. They promise significant results, fulfillment, and accomplishments that everyone gets to share. The promise needs to be bold and audacious. It's either exceptional or not worth listening to.

Great stories are believable. Credibility is a scarce resource and very easy to lose. That's why it is important to show proof of wins along the way. Keep the actual results in front of your audience.

Great stories don't reveal all the details. It is often best to leave some things to the imagination. Some people will dream even bigger dreams than you.

Great stories make great first impressions. If you have to keep selling the story in order to make it sound good, you lose the power of first impressions.

Great stories are repeated by others. Not only do you tell your story, but excited listeners repeat the story, and the effect is multiplied.

Great stories appeal to emotions. Not everything we do is logical. Our stories should also have a personal emotional hook. A great story will stir up the emotions of the audience, and it always gets a response.

Great stories are targeted. Great writers don't necessarily tell stories for a universal audience. When I speak to church planters, I like to tell stories about other church planters. The same stories wouldn't have as much meaning at a gathering of LSU fans. But a great story about a historic LSU victory or a favorite coach would hit the spot.

Great stories are targeted to readers of a specific interest, disposition, or state in life. Still, we need to involve all the characters in our stories, not only the target group but our current congregations too. You'll want to engage everyone in realizing the vision.

Great stories resonate with the audience's beliefs. Great stories change people. They motivate and encourage people to change. They resonate with what the reader/viewer/listener already believes while reminding him how he *knows* he ought to think, live, love, and act. Simply telling the truth of how you have been changed will nudge others to make needed changes.

Great stories offer opportunities to buy in. When you tell your story in an effective manner, people will buy into it. Still, the next steps need to be clear. How can they get involved? Who is the contact person? Where can they learn more detailed information? Where can they sign up? Not only do people need to know the next steps, they need to be able to respond immediately. If you share a great story but don't solicit a response, your momentum will die.

Engage others as you create a plan or strategy. No matter how great your ideas, there is always a better one out there. Unless you let others chime in with their ideas, you may never discover the best one.

Whenever I consult with churches and their staffs, I like to get the pastor and his wife to spend the first hour telling their story of how the church was started or how they came to be leaders of the church. Eyes begin to pop open when the staff members hear of the sacrifice, the struggles, and the humor of all that the couple went through to get the church established. It builds respect and appreciation for all the pastor went through and gives the staff a different perspective on the ministry and their position.

Stories—compelling and well told—are part of what draws people to attractional churches.

PART THREE

The Work of the Attractional Church

Chapter Ten

Reaching Beyond the Church Walls

Raised by a devout Catholic mother, I attended church all my young life. As a child I never missed Mass. As a teenager, I would catch the five o'clock service at St. Anthony's because it was only twenty-five minutes long, or else I'd attend the late Sunday service at Louisiana State University. When I got married, at a very young age I might add, my wife and I never missed church.

Children came along, grew to school age, and I became an even more devout church attendee. There were times that I went every weekday and on weekends. Reasoning that more is better, I sought fulfillment in faithful attendance. I listened to the message, went through all the religious motions, and focused intently on the ritual of church.

But nothing happened. In church I felt safe from my sins but knew it wouldn't last; sooner or later I would revert to the person I really was. I was never transformed by what I heard, what I saw, or what I participated in. Not yet.

But in 1973, I met Christ in my bedroom in a powerful way. As I mentioned earlier, I had borrowed my neighbor's Bible to gain information I could use to convince a professing atheist that there really was a God. In the process, I met Christ.

Then I began attending Bethany Baptist Church in Baker,

Louisiana, and I loved it! Pastor Roy Stockstill had a contagious joy and preached a life-giving word. The frequent guest speakers brought messages of hope and joy. The great testimonies of God's grace and His power working in the lives of ordinary people kept me on the edge of my seat and hungry for more.

What's more, those messages transformed me.

I felt as if I was a part of what God wanted to do in the earth, and that He was preparing me to be used to do great things in His kingdom. I was given new life. Remarkably, everyone who attended felt the same way.

Real transformation motivates us to embrace what we hear to the point of obedience, giving us new life. We are changed. The old person is gone; the new person has come (see 2 Cor. 5:17).

What I see in the most successful attractional churches is a passionate strategy to reach the lost and make disciples rather than have an emotional experience. The entire focus is on how to reach the next soul through God's wisdom; therefore, the pastors avoid the ups and downs of trying to produce some kind of emotional high for believers.

Outreach comes first; then, once we get persons through the doors, we want them to stay. We want them to be changed forever by the presence and power of God. Success is measured by the number of souls more than by physical manifestations.

Outreach, Inreach, Upreach

Think of what we're doing at church as a triangle: The new converts fellowship with other believers; that fellowship aids in discipleship; effective discipleship equips believers for evangelism, which brings more converts into the fold. Then together we all worship and adore the Father. We can also think of this as ***outreach*** (to unbelievers or underchurched), ***inreach*** (to believers within the church), and ***upreach*** (to God).

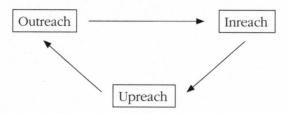

Let's begin with a church's *outreach*. Some aspects of ministry that fall under outreach include evangelism, missions, community service projects—even advertising and marketing campaigns through postcards, billboards, and the Web.

Outreach and the Lost, the Absent, and the Unfulfilled

Ever start a project with certain expectations of what the end product would look like, but the result was not at all what you wanted? Churches can be that way.

They start out with great visions of reaching entire cities. But after a few years they get relegated to an isolated part of town and languish with small numbers, lack of finances, and disgruntled leaders. They come in with an idea of shaping their town into a Christ-honoring city where spiritual awakening is sweeping the thoughts and actions of a majority of the population. Instead of the church shaping the city, however, the city shapes the church. It's tough, disheartening, and frustrating to thousands of churches across America.

So how do we change the culture of a city to be more Christlike? Too often, our idealism leads us down an unrealistic pathway. Our expectations are far more than our outcomes, and our dream is shattered into a million pieces.

Think of your outreach ministry as soil: Whatever you mix in it, how you cultivate it, and what seeds you plant will determine what you get out of it.

Reaching the Lost

With a majority of Americans living without Christ and yet having a desire to find God somewhere, somehow, we have the perfect opportunity to reach them via the attractional church. Give the lost the gospel in a relevant, clear, and powerful way, and they will embrace it. People need God and they know it, so let's give them the God of the Bible in a life-giving way so they will come into the kingdom.

Typical outreach programs have usually featured a sort of street evangelism modeled on the early church. But our lives today are not lived in the town square or the open-air market. We live behind walls and computer screens. Our outreach methods must meet the lost where they are.

The biggest question I would have if we asked believers to take to the streets is, How many of us would actually go do this? What percentage of the body of Christ in America today would actually spend their free time walking in the neighborhoods preaching Christ and ministering to the needs of people? How many slammed doors would it take before these foot soldiers eventually gave up? How many would never even venture out?

Could it be that the reason we do things the way we do today is because our culture dictates it to us? The fact that we have dinner meetings with people, invite them to Sunday church services, and share with them on the golf course should speak to the nature of the culture that we are trying to reach. Are these the best ways? I'm not sure, but they do fit our culture.

The Absent

People who have left church would come back if they could discover the life of an attractional church. It was a lack of life or some conflict that drove them away, but I believe they really desire to renew their faith. Just as Israel disobeyed God and stopped serving Him, once they rediscovered His plan for their lives they returned and were restored. Those who once were in church will always have a flame burning in their hearts that tells them to come back.

So many people are absent from church because of past experiences that turned them off. Conflict, legalism, or pastors failing morally caused them to lose interest and leave. Then there are the hypocrites. They seem to be everywhere. But the honest and sincere Christians are far more in abundance and can help bring the absent back to church.

The most effective way to get people back to church is to start a relationship with them around an interest they have. It could be sports, hobbies, or just about anything they like to talk about. Once you show interest in the things people like, it is easier to get them to want to share in the things you like.

Small, interest-based groups are the perfect place to bring people with whom you have begun relationships. It's not church, but it is the back door to church. Once they come to your group and meet other people they actually enjoy being around, they begin to open up to coming back to church...your church. It is much easier to get them to come because now they know several others who attend and don't feel alone or isolated.

Starting relationships with those who quit church is the first and most basic step to getting them back in church. But there are other means. Many absent believers will go to church on your website or respond to an interesting postcard that offers something different from their grandmother's church. Some people come to attractional churches when they see billboards that advertise messages about controversial subjects in church like sex, divorce, or family problems. One congregation got a lot of response when they labeled themselves "A church for people who hate church."

The Unfulfilled

There's an argument that one church should not attempt to lure other Christians out of the churches that they already attend. If there are problems in their church, let them sort those out on their own so they don't infect your church. Many times, this cross-contagion does happen. But many others are so frustrated with the lack of life in their church that they give up on church altogether. Do we leave them alone or do we reach out and offer them something better?

It comes down to this: Does everyone, Christian and non-Christian, deserve a life-giving church? Does everyone deserve the opportunity to attend a vibrant, empowering church where they can find the presence of God? Should they have a place where they can find fruitful ministry and a place they can bring their friends and family? Do they deserve to find a safe environment to hear the gospel of Christ?

I believe the answer to all these questions is yes. If we can provide such a place where we can reach each person's circle of friends, we will see a great harvest for the Lord.

So what can we do to create a life-giving environment? And if we do it, will people leave their own stagnant churches to experience a life-giving church? I believe people who are unfulfilled in their present church should do whatever is necessary to find fulfillment in a local church.

But many people think church is still the boring service they attended with their parents and grandparents. And there are reasons why they perceive church in this way.

We saw earlier that millions of Christians are staying home these days. The reasons are many. There is, however, a greater number of people who are present but not fulfilled. They are faithful to attend every week, give financially, sing the songs, pray and hope for better things. What do they hope for? To find the things that brought them to church to begin with. Hope, freedom, peace, friends, encouragement—the list goes on. In interviews, Christians named the following things that they're seeking but not finding:

Spiritual encounters. People want an encounter of the God kind. They have tried all the positive thinking, meditation, inward-looking, ancient, and new-age remedies for what ails them, but nothing works. People want God! They want to feel a real God in their hearts and minds and experiences. We don't base our faith on these feelings, but an encounter with Him is what we want nevertheless. God meets with His church throughout the New Testament and continues to meet with His church today. Let's give Him room to do so. It is the church's responsibility to help people connect with God through worship, fellowship, the Word, and prayer.

Connection with people. "No one greeted or welcomed us, and we are new to town." No one likes to be lonely. Everyone wants interaction with other people who can understand their situation, relate to their issues, and be part of their lives.

Recreational involvement. "We wanted to get involved with other Christians in things outside of church, but it just didn't happen." I am not a big proponent of avoiding the world for the sake of Christ. But there are times when I just want to hang out with believers, where we can encourage one another and share all that Christ is doing in our lives. Some churches are great at providing these kinds of opportunities, but many are not.

Children's development. "The kids learned a few songs but were mostly unchanged by coming."

Opportunities to serve in areas of special interest. "No one seemed to be interested in what we had to offer."

Teaching that's relevant to real-life issues. "Even after being in church for years, I don't know any more about how to do life than I did before I started."

Leadership. "We wanted someone to guide us in biblical principles for life. We were looking for strong leadership but found that the leaders served only the corporation and not the people."

Counseling in life issues such as relationships. "We needed help with our marriage and our teenagers. They had no answers, much less compassion."

Worship and music. "I heard this music fifteen years ago—same old worn-out choruses. No one seemed to be worshipping the Lord."

Business and political connections. "I wanted to connect with the business community in the church. It was difficult to find businesspeople who could relate to us."

Hope. "I am looking for something that will make my life better and give me hope in these tough times." If people are coming for this reason, they'd better find it at church. For many people, church is the last resort to find hope in the midst of pain and suffering. Unfortunately, many seeking hope find condemnation instead.

Freedom from guilt, obligation, and duty. "I feel more guilt and more hopeless than before I started going to church. I thought God wanted to forgive me, not just give me more impossible rules."

Involvement of spouse. "I brought my husband, hoping he would get engaged. He didn't. He says he won't go back."

Faithful role models. "I work with some of the people in the church I visited. I would not want to live like them. Seems like no one there lives a godly life that I would want to emulate."

Understanding. "I need to figure out some issues in my life. I'm just trying to make some sense of it all." God's instructions for living are revealed in the living Bible—and churches should make the Word understandable and clear.

Purpose/significance. "At this point in my life, I need a bigger purpose for living. There has to be more to life than the nine-to-five." Many people have found success in business and other pursuits, yet life feels empty. What greater purpose than the cause of Christ?

Status/reputation. "My parents' church helped them build a strong reputation in town. I remember people used to say, 'He's a good man. He goes to that church.' It meant a lot to be known as a churchgoer." These days, churchgoing has lost its status for some, but for others it speaks of a person who lives a life of faith and commitment. Commitment to something beyond your own interests speaks volumes about your status in the community. When you're committed to charities, causes, and the local church, it adds to your status or reputation.

A contemporary church experience. "My family used to go to this church, but it seems so outdated now." When churches fall behind the times, parents and children lose interest. The local church simply must understand the times and culture of today's youth and provide relevant ministry to younger generations. Families will remain together in church if their needs are addressed. This requires that young ministers be raised up and allowed to minister alongside the pastor.

People come to church for different reasons, and they really do want to connect. But they are not finding what they need. Make a checklist of the needs I've just listed, and ask yourself if you're meeting these needs in your local church. Where you find gaps, make a plan and a conscious effort to effect changes. You will be amazed at how quickly things will turn around and how your church will begin to grow.

People are looking for fulfillment in their church and God experience. Too often, they get lengthy sermons, plenty of religion, a number of activities—and they are still empty. Still hungry. People don't get the spiritual nutrition they need to take root and grow.

The good news is that nourishment can be found in attractional churches. I have dedicated the rest of my life to starting life-giving churches—churches that offer relationships, hope, understanding, purpose, and an encounter with the living God. Let's join together to see this become a reality.

Chapter Eleven

Permission Evangelism

The attractional church has learned effective evangelism by attracting unchurched people to its Sunday services. By creating an environmentally safe place to bring their friends and relatives, its members bring visitors every week. We record thousands of salvations every year in our Sunday services. Even though this is an effective method of evangelism, it cannot replace the need for individual Christians to know how to share Christ effectively. The fact is, millions of people in America will never attend a local church service. So it is vitally important to develop skills for winning people to Christ if we are ever going to reach the masses of unchurched people in our country. Learning how to share Christ is of utmost importance.

The most effective way to communicate the gospel to an unbeliever is not through force, imposition, or insult—something I call *confrontational evangelism*. Rather, communicating the gospel when we are "given permission" yields much better results. Teaching and practicing permission evangelism is an important component in the outreach ministry of the attractional church.

The greatest tragedy in life is when a person dies without knowing Christ. We all need to be prepared to do the work of a disciple—to teach non-Christians who Jesus is and why they need to have a relationship with him. In this chapter you'll learn practical steps to share the most important message of all, the good news of Jesus Christ.

In 2 Timothy 4:5, Paul encourages Timothy and members of the church to "do the work of an evangelist" (NIV). As you read this, you may be questioning whether Paul was talking to you. You may argue that your gifting lies in leadership or administration or pastoring—but not in evangelism.

Although we do not all have the gift of eloquent speaking, God did give us the ability to share Christ. The truth is, as believers, we all are expected to tell others about our lives in Christ and how our lives have changed since becoming a Christian. Paul asks, "How, then, can they call on the one they have not believed in? And how can they believe in the one of whom they have not heard? And how can they hear without someone preaching to them?" (Rom. 10:14 NIV).

What Is Evangelism, Anyway?

You are doing the work of an evangelist when you invite a nonbelieving friend to worship, church, small group, or another church social function. You're an evangelist when you take the time to pray with a friend, or when you share Christ as you serve others through community outreach. Evangelism is the practice of sharing the good news in ways that help connect people to Christ and to church.

Through conversation with friends, family, or acquaintances, you can share the goodness of Christ. Present the gospel by sharing your personal testimony, reading Scripture with people, or discussing how Christ can help them in their lives.

In addition to sharing the gospel verbally, you can evangelize through simple acts. The way you live your life is the best way to convey the work of the Holy Spirit in you. Let your everyday actions be your strongest evangelistic tool. Matthew wrote, "Let your light shine before men, that they may see your good deeds and praise your Father in heaven" (Matt. 5:16 NIV).

Don't be intimidated when it comes to speaking about God or sharing Scriptures with others. Even though we have received the power of the Holy Spirit in our lives, we may sometimes feel unworthy or incapable of evangelizing others. Remember, as we've read in the Great Commission, it is our responsibility as Christians to share how others can receive a new life in Christ. Through the power of the Holy Spirit, we can overcome our timidity and any ambivalence in sharing our testimony and faith. God gives us the power, knowledge, confidence, and words we need to be an effective witness for Jesus:

> "When you are brought before synagogues, rulers and authorities, do not worry about how you will defend yourselves or what you will say, for the Holy Spirit will teach you at that time what you should say" (Luke 12:11–12 NIV).

As I've mentioned, *permission evangelism* is a productive way to share the gospel. It involves developing relationships with people to gain their permission before you share the gospel. Through one-on-one ministry, group meetings, and other events, Jesus and His disciples shared the gospel in a way that captured the hearts and minds of the people. As miracles and healings took place, people opened up to the message of the gospel and often begged to hear more. The results of permission evangelism are likely to be more positive than with confrontational evangelism because you first gain the other person's permission, approval, or consent to share. And you gain that permission through dynamic spiritual relationships.

Dynamic Spiritual Relationships: Easy as E-I-E-I-O

E: Encircle

The first step in building a relationship is to encircle people with prayer. Pray daily for opportunities to meet them and for appropriate circumstances to talk with them about your life in Christ.

There are so many people with whom we can develop dynamic spiritual relationships. We can reach out to family, friends, coworkers, neighbors, and acquaintances. Anyone we show mercy to can be considered a neighbor; therefore, we can share the love of Christ with them.

The most important thing you can do is pray. Pray for people to come out of the darkness and into the light; for your own personal boldness; for protection, safety, and trust around people you want to evangelize; against any attack of the enemy on those persons.

Paul tells us, "The god of this age has blinded the minds of unbelievers, so that they cannot see the light of the gospel of the glory of Christ, who is the image of God" (2 Cor. 4:4 NIV). Ask God to open their eyes, ears, and hearts to prepare them to hear the message. As you speak to them, be sure to stress that the only way to God the Father is through Jesus.

Prayer will...

- prepare your heart to build a dynamic spiritual relationship with others.
- open opportunities for you to minister to and evangelize others.
- tear down the walls of demonic obstruction, spiritual blindness, and diversion.
- build trust between you and others; they will likely open up to you without intimidation or resentment.
- fill your heart with love for other people. Your compassion and concern will break down barriers and cause them to respond.

I: Invite

Evangelism doesn't have to take place in a church setting. It can happen anywhere. Choose a comfortable, relaxed, or fun setting and show others hospitality. Invite them to your home, the coffee shop, the golf course, the park, a social event—anyplace they would enjoy and where they would feel comfortable and at ease. They need to see you and other Christians interact away from the church.

It doesn't matter so much where you go; the goal is to provide an opportunity for the Holy Spirit to do something in others' lives. It is important, however, to make sure the occasions to which you invite people have a spiritual element; otherwise, there will be no spiritual fruit. During your time together, look for an opportunity to interject God's answer to one of their problems. You can also share your own testimony with them or tell them about the blessings of God in your life.

Look for ways to serve others by meeting an obvious need. Find out if there is something you can do to help them or their family. Do they have a home improvement project with which you could lend a hand? Is someone in their family ill? Perhaps you could take dinner to help them out.

After your initial outing, extend another invitation, this time to a small group. This will help the persons get acquainted with other Christians in a nonthreatening environment. Find a topic that interests them and draw them into the conversation. As they get to know members of the small group, they'll be developing the support system they'll need once they accept Christ.

Once the persons have visited the small group, they'll be more open to visiting your church and to furthering relationships they've already established.

E: Enlist

As you persist in prayer and invitations, the day may come when the people you're interacting with finally open their hearts to salvation. Once they have made a decision for the Lord, it will be time to enlist and engage them in service to God and others.

- Help them find an appropriate small group to join.
- Bring them to church.
- Get them enrolled in a new believers' class.
- Encourage them to be baptized in water.

As newborn babes in Christ, new believers will need care, which is the next step in the process.

I: Intern

Internship often refers to work performed in order to gain practical experience. In the Christian context, the intern process is called *discipleship*. All new believers need people to help them walk through the practical steps of Christianity.

Once people come to a saving knowledge of the Lord Jesus, they need to learn to live and abide in Christ. They need to mature as believers. In practical terms, they must learn to respond like Christ in difficult situations, pray for their enemies, face and overcome sin, recognize the voice of God, and understand the Scriptures.

The process of internship takes the new believer from being a totally dependent child of faith to becoming a spiritually mature adult who cares for others. It transforms the believer's salvation from that of a great and glorious short-term experience to a lifestyle.

During this procedure, be sure to have ongoing contact with new believers. Give them a telephone call every now and then. Ask them out for coffee to catch up with the events of their week. Make sure they are becoming disciples.

O: Obligate

The last step of converting a new believer into a fully devoted follower of Christ is to obligate that person into continuing the discipleship process by reaching out to others and bringing them to a relationship with Christ. Disciples are obligated to make other disciples.

God will place an urging in new believers' hearts to reach out to their own families and friends; they will desire to share the love of Christ and the new life that comes with that love. They will be on their way to fulfilling their roles in the Great Commission, our responsibility to preach the gospel to all the world. They'll also restart the cycle of developing new dynamic spiritual relationships.

How Do We Gain "Permission"?

For permission evangelism to work, we need to learn to recognize a heart that is open to hearing the gospel. There are times when people are openly asking us to share our beliefs and talk about our relationships with Christ—and we don't even know it. Quite often, unbelievers and seekers open the door for us to share Christ with them without expressing that desire in words. For some, an invitation for us to witness to them can be found in their actions or conversations.

Always look for an occasion to share the gospel with someone, whether that someone is a friend, a relative, or a recent acquaintance. God gives us divine appointments, and we need to be alert and able to recognize the opportunities He gives us to share our faith.

You have permission to share your faith...

When people walk into your church. In 1 Corinthians 14:24–25, we see an example of unbelievers coming to Christ during a church service: "If an unbeliever or someone who does not understand comes in while everybody is prophesying, he will be convinced by all that he is a sinner and will be judged by all, and the secrets of his heart will be laid bare. So he will fall down and worship God, exclaiming, 'God is really among you!'" (NIV).

If a friend or stranger comes to a regular church service, he is in essence giving you permission to share the gospel with him. Therefore, you can feel free to reinforce the message. Ask specific questions to gauge his understanding, and invite him to respond to the offer of salvation.

When people use religion to justify their actions or lifestyles. Have you ever heard people claim membership to a religious organization or affiliation when confronted with sin or inconsistencies in their lifestyles? People often try to hide behind a religious facade to justify themselves and their behavior. They know that their lives are not right, and they're embarrassed to admit it.

When they say, "I have personal beliefs," or "I was raised by religious parents," or "I do go to church!" you have their permission to ask them about their spiritual lives. Sometimes they will openly admit that they have been away from God but desire to rekindle their spirituality. The goal is not to show them their hypocrisy, but rather to lead them to a spiritual life that supersedes religion.

When people have questions about life's trials. The world's system cannot offer real solutions to life's trials; only God can. In

Scripture we have the assurance that through Christ, we can over-come any hardship or difficulty: "I can do all things through Christ who strengthens me" (Phil. 4:13 NKJV).

The message that Jesus Christ came to give us life and life more abundantly (see John 10:10) will forever be a relevant message to people who have questions about the trials they are enduring. We should feel free to share Christ with anyone who is struggling with life's problems.

When people try to justify their sinful lifestyles. Have you ever heard people brag about "joining their friends in hell" when they die? If so, you should use that opportunity to express your joy in joining your friends and Jesus in heaven. People may jokingly talk about going to hell without realizing the gravity of their com-ments. When they bring up the subject of an afterlife, you have permission to tell them about eternal life in Jesus.

When people desire a relationship with you. In various parts of your social and professional life, you have opportunities to develop friendships. Regardless of how it begins, if a person is willing to get to know you and open up to you, you've got an open door to communicating the gospel truth to him.

When people ask for help or advice. It is one thing when we as Christians approach a person cold turkey and attempt to share Christ. It is quite another thing when someone comes to us for help or advice. We should look at this as an open invitation to share the source of all real help, Jesus Christ.

When people ask about your faith. Chances are that you've been asked, "How can you be so happy?" or "Where do you get your strength to get through difficult times?" When someone approaches you this way, you have gained permission to tell him or her about the source of all real joy, Jesus Christ.

When people respond to a sermon. Altar calls invite individu-als to receive Christ or to come forward for specific prayer needs. When people respond to the call and approach the altar, they have given permission to have Christ shared with them. In churches where there are no altar calls, people may respond to any other invitation to accept Christ or receive prayer. Be sure to let them know that regardless of their past sins, those sins can be forgiven because Christ died for them.

When people respond to mail-outs. Churches sometimes send out a general mailing to the community to provoke response from individuals who may have interest in the church. When people respond, you have permission to contact them. Once you respond to their inquiries, if you see evidence of further interest, you may gain permission to move to the next step, which may be to share Christ with them.

When people give interviews for surveys. Many churches use door-to-door surveys about spiritually related matters to locate people who are open to hearing the gospel. If you find people who will take the time to answer questions, you also have an opportunity to ask about their relationships with Christ. You might ask, "What do you think the Bible teaches about how to get to heaven?" Once they respond, ask if you may share Christ with them—that's your permission.

When people come for counseling. One of the greatest services offered by churches is godly counsel. When people approach a Christian or Christian counselor for advice and guidance, and if they confide in you about a problem, they are giving you permission to speak about the power of the Holy Spirit. You also have permission to address sin they may be struggling with or anything that is keeping a person away from Christ.

When people fill out a visitor's card. Most churches make cards available for newcomers to complete. These cards are useful in obtaining a newcomer's information and prayer requests. If a person also gives permission to be contacted, by all means do so.

When people's children come to Christ. Whether in Sunday school, through a parent, at a camp, or in a small-group setting, most of us came to Christ early in life. As people get older, the chances of their getting saved grows less probable. So when a child gives his life to Christ, you have a great opportunity to share Christ with his parents too.

My Own Experiences with Permission Evangelism

I have used permission evangelism throughout my Christian life. Charlene and I would invite couples over for dinner. With most of these couples the husband was not a believer but would go along with the wife to have dinner with the pastor. After sharing a wonderful dinner together, I would take the husband in another room to show him something he might be interested in. It could be old watches or my gun collection. After a while, when I felt comfortable with him, I would ask if he had a religious background.

Most of the time the man would tell me about his church upbringing, then admit he had lost interest in church and still had questions about God. My next step was to ask permission to talk with him about his questions. Once we were conversing, I looked for opportunities to share my testimony as it related to his struggles and eventually share the gospel. I led many men to Christ in my hobby room.

Another opportunity I had to share Christ came was when I was a Louisiana state policeman. At the scene of an accident or while issuing a ticket for speeding, I would often just ask drivers how their lives were going and if there was anything they would like to talk about off the record. Many times they would begin to share their struggles and right there, in full uniform, I would share the love of God and the gospel of Christ with them. It was very effective.

One of the most memorable events occurred when I came upon a pickup truck stopped on the interstate. I saw a man sitting on the tailgate with blood gushing from his chest. A teenage boy was with him and I asked the teen what had happened. He said, "He has been shot!"

"Who shot him?"

"I did."

The wounded man had been beating this teenager's mom and

the boy shot the man, his stepfather, point-blank in the chest with a .357 Magnum revolver—one of the most deadly handguns in existence at the time. It wasn't difficult for me to get permission to share Christ with this dying man in the back of the pickup truck as he fell over and began to lose consciouness. We prayed to receive Christ and I prayed that God would spare his life....God did and he went home from the hospital a few days after being shot.

There are many times in life when people are ready to listen and will give you the opportunity to share Jesus Christ with them. Just be on the alert.

How to Get Started? Just "Dare" to Share

Use the acrostic "DARE" to effectively communicate four major points of the gospel message.

D refers to the fact that Christ *died* for our sins: "You see, at just the right time, when we were still powerless, Christ died for the ungodly. Very rarely will anyone die for a righteous man, though for a good man someone might possibly dare to die. But God demonstrates his own love for us in this: While we were still sinners, Christ died for us" (Rom. 5:6–8 NIV).

A: When you *accept* Christ, He accepts you. When you receive Him as Lord, He receives you into His kingdom.

R: To *repent* is to turn away from sin and turn to Christ for righteousness.

E: Christ gives us *eternal* life when we believe in Him. According to the Scriptures: "God so loved the world that he gave his one and only Son, that whoever believes in him shall not perish but have eternal life" (John 3:16 NIV).

After you have shared the four major aspects of becoming a Christian, ask the person if he believes that Jesus died for his sins and rose from the dead according to Romans 10:9. Ask, "Are you ready to accept the wonderful gift God has given you?" If the answer is yes, you have not only permission but the privilege of praying with him for salvation!

Permission evangelism has been a very effective way to reach the underchurched for years. Having a basic inderstanding of when people are actually giving you permission to share Christ will take the hesitancy and fear out of evangelism.

The Lost: Accept the Outsider

Effective inreach, being transformed into the image of Jesus, helps us become more effective in outreach. Jesus accepted sinners, impacted their lives, forgave them, and sent them on their way forever changed for the better. Acceptance does not mean approving the lifestyles of lost people, but respecting them as people and inviting them to hear the gospel so that they will come to Christ. Following Jesus were prostitutes, thieves, religious hypocrites, and various other sinners who numbered in the thousands. He never made the "sinners" leave; rather, He just kept preaching the good news of the kingdom until they became believers. This is outreach.

But what do we do with the world? you may be wondering. A life-giving church exists to reach the lost, the absent, and the unfulfilled. It all starts with the lost. Outside our walls is a world without Christ, and it's our job to reach them and offer the life of God that is in Jesus Christ. In Lamentations 3:22 we are encouraged, "Because of the LORD's great love we are not consumed, for his compassions never fail" (NIV). Christ had compassion on us all, and He died on the cross to show that compassion. What's more, He instructs us to have that same compassion for the world. We are compelled to reach out to a hurting world with the love of Jesus.

But what about the warning to keep our distance from the unrighteous? Let's look at exactly what Scripture says before we visit the dark world of the unbeliever (keeping in mind it was once our world too, and would be still, if not for the grace of God).

Look at what the apostle Paul says to the Corinthian church:

Be ye not unequally yoked together with unbelievers: for what fellowship hath righteousness with unrighteousness? and what communion hath light with darkness? And what concord hath Christ with Belial? or what part hath he that believeth with an infidel? And what agreement hath the temple of God with idols? for ye are the temple of the living God; as God hath said, I will dwell in them, and walk in them; and I will be their God, and they shall be my people. Wherefore come out from among them, and be ye separate, saith the Lord, and touch not the unclean thing; and I will receive you. And will be a Father unto you, and ye shall be my sons and daughters, saith the Lord Almighty (2 Corinthians 6:14–18 KJV).

Light has no fellowship with darkness: "Come out from among them"; "Touch not the unclean thing." These are strong words about our involvement with the world—and they sound even more forbidding in the King James Bible. But how can we be holy and separate from the world and yet reach the same world for Christ?

If we are to avoid these unclean people, who will reach them? Let's take a closer look.

Do Not Be Unequally Yoked

According to *Strong's Exhaustive Concordance*, the phrase "unequally yoked together" is the translation of just one Greek word, *hetero-zugeo*, which is a compound word that means "to yoke up differently; to associate discordantly; unequally yoke together."[1] It is used but this one time in the Bible.

The meaning here is to not be yoked with a different kind of person or, according to *Strong's Exhaustive Concordance*, to not be yoked with a "beast" of a different kind. It literally means, in this case, to not have intercourse with unbelievers. Of course that would require marriage in the first place. So Paul is saying, "Do not be in relationship or marry unbelievers where there will be eventual intercourse with them."

We are urged, however, to reach out to them with love and

compassion. We are not to walk in their ways but to show them a better way, to lead them out of darkness and into light. We are not to become like them, but rather help them become like Christ as we are like Christ.

I believe the key phrase in 2 Corinthians 6:14 is "Be ye not unequally yoked together with unbelievers" (KJV). In our quest to reach the world for Christ, we will have to befriend them, share life with them, share truth with them, and even put up with some of their worldliness—but we don't have to be yoked up to what they are yoked up to. Jesus has set us free, and by all means we must stay free.

Let's reach them with the power of love and righteousness, snatching them out of the fire...without being burned.

As Christians, we are called by the Lord to a relationship of reconciliation with those in the world, but we do not have to subject ourselves to its pressures. We are in the world but not of the world (see John 17:14–15).

Chapter Twelve

A Church That Looks Like Jesus

For us to have effective outreach to our families, friends, and the world around us, we will need to also have effective *inreach* to our church members. Inreach applies to ministries that may include teaching, discipleship, benevolence, counseling, and the like. Inreach equips the saints to glorify God and do the work of ministry.

In 1 Peter 2:9–10 we see what God has called the church to and what we should aspire to: "You are a chosen people, a royal priesthood, a holy nation, a people belonging to God, that you may declare the praises of him who called you out of darkness into his wonderful light. Once you were not a people, but now you are the people of God; once you had not received mercy, but now you have received mercy" (NIV).

This is who we are as the church of Jesus Christ: a chosen, holy people who are priests unto God. We practice inreach when we focus on being transformed into the likeness of Jesus so that our lives declare His praises.

We must lead our churches back to the person of Jesus Christ and His attributes. A church that looks like Jesus is what this country needs. Pastor Chris Hodges puts it like this: "It is not so much what we *do* but who we *are* that will make the difference." *Who we are* should reflect the glory of God. Only then will *what we do* move the hearts of the lost world toward Jesus and His church.

Once we have the heart of Jesus and realize that as His chosen people our job is to reach those He died for, church takes on a whole new meaning. A new discussion takes place. What is the center of interest at your church? Attractional churches focus on being life-giving to the lost and generous in all they do, and building a leadership base that will care for the growth that will come.

Inreach prepares our hearts to do outreach. When we walk in the footsteps of Jesus and become more like Him, we are more effective reaching the world around us. As we become more like Jesus we will be more accepting of others, more sensitive to their needs, and more understanding of the world that is without Jesus.

Generosity to All

As our hearts are transformed to be like Christ, a giving spirit will be the end result. Contrary to the "me first" mind-set that prevails in America, generosity to others must take precedence in our lives. Living in a self-centered society full of greed and ambition, we know it's difficult to stay focused on the needs of others. Even as Christians, we sometimes live for ourselves and take advantage of people to get ahead. Too often, pastors and church leadership are more focused on what they can get instead of what they can give. To create attractional churches, we have to get back to the spirit of Christ in the area of giving. "You are familiar with the generosity of our Master, Jesus Christ. Rich as he was, he gave it all away for us—in one stroke he became poor and we became rich" (2 Cor. 8:9 The Message).

This is the Spirit of Christ. He gave it all up, Paul says. Though he was rich, for our sakes He entered into the poverty of human existence and held absolutely nothing back, not even His own life. We remember this each time we gather at the Lord's Table. There on the hill of Calvary, on a rugged, bloody, cruel cross, He poured out everything He had. John puts it in one phrase full of implications: "Having loved his own which were in the world, he loved them unto the end" (John 13:1 KJV). *That* is giving. That is what Paul is talking about. No reserves, no half-measures, no conditions, no holding back, but pouring out everything we have for others.

That is the great pattern of giving. We've never really given until it costs us something.

We've all heard the message of stewardship and tithing from the pulpit. But the best message is one we see modeled by our leaders. Dino Rizzo at Healing Place Church always speaks of putting the needy first in his community. He talks often of generosity and sacrificial giving. He had his chance to model this when Katrina hit New Orleans. The people of Louisiana were devastated by the impact of that cruel storm. What did the church do about it?

Pastor Dino Rizzo was one of the founding members of PRC Compassion. Gene Mills, PRC Compassion's president wrote this about their work together:

> In the wake of Hurricane's Katrina and Rita, Healing Place Church has given almost $1,500,000. As a major partner in PRC Compassion, we were able to deliver over $65,000,000 in in-kind donations. [PRC Compassion is an organization that helped pool resources that came in from churches around the United States to help in the relief effort.] This included 65,000,000 pounds of resources from 1,900 truckloads. HPC directed over 1,000 volunteers and hosted shelters at the Donaldsonville and Spanish campus.
>
> Because of your generosity, PRC Compassion has been able to achieve more than anyone ever dreamed. PRC has directed four hundred semitrucks to eighteen distribution points throughout Louisiana, housed and fed over six hundred out-of-state volunteers that have come to serve the hurting, distributed thousands of cots to shelters all over the state, and housed and fed over ten thousand displaced citizens. These are just a few things that have been accomplished thus far, and we are now able to continue Hurricane Katrina relief efforts, as well as begin to help those affected by Hurricane Rita. As I write this, we already have teams reaching out to hard-hit areas in Lake Charles, Louisiana, and Beaumont, Texas.[1]

It is amazing what the body of Christ can do when its members come together.

The Multiplication of Leaders

Jesus' example of effective leadership is to be our model for the attractional church. Good leaders have a servant's heart (see Luke 12:37) and are friends to sinners (see Matt. 11:19; Luke 7:34). Jesus was the greatest multiplier of leaders ever. He developed them to be the ones who would take the message of the kingdom to the world. His *inreach* to the men he wanted to lead equipped them to do even greater works than He did while on earth. It was His plan.

A God-seeking leader who desires growth for his congregation will be single-minded in his dedication to following His Father's will (see John 5:19). Jesus was committed to every detail of what the Father wanted Him to do and how He was to do it.

Jesus was also powerful. It is only through God's power that we can accomplish the task of changing the world for Him. Jesus said, "Anyone who believes in me will do the same works I have done, and even greater works, because I am going to be with the Father" (John 14:12 NLT). It would be impossible for us to accomplish "greater works" without His power, so He sent the Holy Spirit to enable us. When we capture the power of God in our everyday lives, the result could be an astounding revival in the United States and around the world.

Once we have the nature of Christ in us, and our lives reflect God's attributes, then we have an attractional church—then we can carry out His Great Commission.

Paul wrote about inreach in 2 Timothy 2:2: "The things you have heard me say in the presence of many witnesses entrust to reliable men who will also be qualified to teach others" (NIV). It was the apostle Paul's desire that Timothy would take the doctrine and wisdom shared with him and pass it along to reliable men who would, in turn, share it with others. For churches to reach their attracting potential, their members must grow and develop in the area of leadership. As leaders are taught, trained, and empowered, they will train others. The base of your leadership structure will begin to broaden and deepen, giving your church a stronger foundation for the increase of many people.

The greatest benefit of multiplying leaders is for the leaders themselves. They feel that value has been added to their lives and that they are now more productive in the kingdom of God and therefore fulfilling their purpose in life. Effective inreach, development of leaders, equals ongoing outreach.

And what is that purpose?

It's enjoying the fruit of a life that chases after God—the *upreach* of the church. We'll talk about that next.

Upreach: A Life That Chases After God

In Paul's sermon at Antioch in Acts 13:22 NKJV, he briefly recounts a statement made by God concerning David: "I have found David, the son of Jesse, a man after my own heart who will do all my will." This is a picture of someone who is totally sold out, not just to the mission of God, but to the person of God. It's no wonder that David penned so many of the Psalms that worship God in such a beautiful way. David's attitude toward God is an attitude we should all have; it's an attitude of pursuit of initmacy with the Holy God. In Psalm 119:97 NIV he says "Oh how I love your Law! I meditate on it all day long." David's affection for God's law reveals how closely related God's Word is to his Person. It gave him great peace of mind during conflict and courage in battle. He knew it was the strength he needed for victory. We show our affection to God in many ways, but first by hiding his word in our heart. David said in Psalm 1:2 NIV "But his delight is in the law of the Lord and on his law he meditates day and night." Another way that we express upreach to God is prayer, and prayer is based upon the fact that it brings God close to us and as Jesus slipped away to pray privately, even in times of his greatest trial, we should also find that secret place where we commune with God in prayer, Psalm 119:64 NIV, "Seven times a day I praise you for your righteous laws." David sang to the Lord and praised him for all that He did and all that He stood for. David reveals his quest after God's heart in that he was willing to do all of God's will as Jesus said in the Garden of Gethsemane, Mark 14:36c NLT "yet I want your will to be done, not mine." This is our upreach to God, that we should totally commit ourselves to knowing Him, worshipping Him, seeking Him in prayer and praising Him for His mighty acts.

Chapter Thirteen

Your Church and the Tree of Life

Persimmons are among my favorite fruits. Down south, you will find this wonderful fruit tree standing mostly unmolested along isolated country roads. If the average person only knew the sweetness of this delicate fruit, he would pull over, climb the farmer's fence, and fill his front seat with them.

Yet when you say "persimmon," most people say, "Uggghh, that's the worst fruit ever!" That's because a persimmon, before it is ripe, is the most bitter thing you've ever tasted. But once it ripens, it's one of the best things you can put in your mouth. It's all a matter of knowing when it is ready to eat.

Jesus said, "Every tree is known by its own fruit" (Luke 6:44 NKJV). A good tree brings forth good fruit and a bad tree brings forth bad fruit. It is pretty easy to judge the fruit of a tree: Just take a bite. Either you will smile and say, "Mmmm, that's good," or you'll spit it out as fast as you can. The same is true of the church. When we bring our guests, they either love it or hate it. Either they walk out enriched with the experience or they're just glad that it's over.

So how does a tree produce good fruit? It all started in the Garden of Eden. And as we grow in Him, Jesus makes the fruit of the tree of life available to us. This is our *upreach*.

The Tree of Life

"The LORD God had planted a garden in the east, in Eden; and there he put the man he had formed. And the LORD God made all kinds of trees grow out of the ground—trees that were pleasing to the eye and good for food. In the middle of the garden were the tree of life and the tree of the knowledge of good and evil" (Gen. 2:8–9 NIV).

Life as we know it today was altered in this place called Eden when Adam and Eve were introduced to the tree of life and the tree of the knowledge of good and evil.

As you may remember, Satan convinced Eve to eat of the tree of the knowledge of good and evil then talked Adam into it. When this happened, they sinned and their eyes were opened to good and evil. They lost their innocence before God and retreated in shame—they hid from their Maker and Friend. They ultimately passed this sin on to all humankind.

The fall of man set up two things: an endless cycle of failure and the eventual offer of righteousness through Jesus Christ. This one act of disobedience still affects us today; it impacts how we live and think and feel.

To make that clear, let me explain a little more about these two trees.

When Adam and Eve sinned in the Garden of Eden, life as man knew it was forever changed:

- Murphy's law was birthed: "Anything that can go wrong will go wrong."
- Mosquitoes and no-see-ums were born.
- Food became fattening.
- Disease was introduced to humankind.
- Spiritual death occurred.
- Humankind was cursed with the inability to please God.
- The wheels of redemption began to turn.

Eating the fruit of the tree of the knowledge of good and evil makes us judgmental, critical, unforgiving, and revengeful. It's all about right and wrong, comparisons and judgments. When we live this way we are constantly accusing others and defending ourselves. We see this in Herod when he had the children in Bethlehem age two years and younger killed because he felt threatened by the new baby-king, Jesus. This spirit of good and evil is also revealed when Herod had John the Baptist beheaded for denouncing his marriage. The critical spirit of the tree of the knowledge of good and evil is extremely problematic to the church, because it ignites self-preservation, self-promotion, and conflict. The opposite is true of the tree of life.

Eating the fruit of the tree of life produces an attitude of acceptance, forgiveness, and empowerment in us. It is the Spirit of Jesus when He forgave the woman caught in adultery, when He visited Zacchaeus in his home and saved him, and when He saw the faith of the centurion and healed his servant. All these stories reveal the heart of a life-giving Servant. Eating the fruit of the tree of life produces healing, reconciliation, and encouragement.

The Tree of Life: Where God Wants Us to Live

Jesus came that we might "have life and have it more abundantly" (John 10:10 NAB). He is all about forgiveness, freedom, and life. When He came He had one thing in mind: to set humankind free from Adam and Eve's sin and the consequences of moral failure. He became the sacrifice for our sins and dealt with them once and for all on the cross. Hebrews says, "Under the old covenant, the priest stands and ministers before the altar day after day, offering the same sacrifices again and again, which can never take away sins. But our High Priest offered himself to God as a single sacrifice for sins, good for all time" (10:11–12 NLT).

The sin debt is settled, and we who accept that sacrifice are forgiven and free and have entered into the life of Christ. We are partakers of the "divine nature," according to 2 Peter, as we live out this new life:

By his divine power, God has given us everything we need for living a godly life. We have received all of this by coming

> to know him, the one who called us to himself by means of his marvelous glory and excellence. And because of his glory and excellence, he has given us great and precious promises. These are the promises that enable you to share his divine nature and escape the world's corruption caused by human desires (2 Peter 1:3–4 NLT).

As we "reach up" to God in worship and hunger for Him and His likeness in our lives, we are transformed.

We are also recipients of promises; according to verse 4, God has given us everything we need for living godly lives. Amazing stuff. Peter reminds us to respond to God's promises and informs us of some supplements we should take as we eat the fruit of the tree of life so we can begin producing the fruit of the Spirit.

> In view of all this, make every effort to respond to God's promises. Supplement your faith with a generous provision of moral excellence, and moral excellence with knowledge, and knowledge with self-control, and self-control with patient endurance, and patient endurance with godliness, and godliness with brotherly affection, and brotherly affection with love for everyone (2 Peter 1:5–7 NLT).

Now we are fully equipped to live out God's promises, enjoy the fruit of the tree of life, and excel in faith as we partake of the salvation that God provides for us through Christ. God spoke to the church in Revelation about the depth of our privileges and rights as heirs of this great kingdom: "He who has an ear, let him hear what the Spirit says to the churches. To him who overcomes, I will give the right to eat from the tree of life, which is in the paradise of God" (Rev. 2:7 NIV).

Because of Jesus, now we have access to the tree of life again. We can feast on life every day and live from the fruit of it. That fruit is made available through the Holy Spirit: "The fruit of the Spirit is love, joy, peace, patience, kindness, goodness, faithfulness, gentleness and self-control" (Gal. 5:22–23 NIV). Knowing this, we should desire to grow in these qualities and partake of the fruit of the Spirit as much as we can.

We have had enough experience with the tree of the knowledge of good and evil to last us several lifetimes. Instead, we can eat fruit from the tree of life and be strengthened in our walk in the Spirit. Jesus is our example of living a life of freedom in the Spirit.

The Local Church That Offers Life

Consider a few Scriptures that define what the local church should be all about. Remember, there were two trees in the Garden of Eden, and it's up to us to choose where we will eat.

"She is a tree of life to those who embrace her; those who lay hold of her will be blessed" (Prov. 3:18 NIV). Who is "she"? Proverbs 3:13 reads, "Happy is the man who finds wisdom" (NKJV). The first fruit from the tree of life that the local church should serve is wisdom. It is in itself a tree of life. "Give me wisdom and knowledge," Solomon said to God, "that I may lead this people" (2 Chron. 1:10 NIV). We need the same from the local church. Our upreach prayer: "Give us wisdom. It is a tree of life to us, and we will be blessed when we receive it."

Next is righteousness. Proverbs 11:30 says, "The fruit of the righteous is a tree of life, and he who wins souls is wise" (NIV). In our efforts at upreach, we should pray, "Teach me how I have been made to be righteousness and what that means in my everyday life." As Paul affirmed, "He hath made him to be sin for us, who knew no sin; that we might be made the righteousness of God in him" (2 Cor. 5:21 KJV). So we pray, "I want to be a tree of life to my children and spouse. I want to touch people with this life so that they will want to know my Savior. This life wins souls, so teach me how to live it, produce it, and share it."

We further read in Proverbs, "Hope deferred makes the heart sick, but a longing fulfilled is a tree of life" (13:12 NIV). A longing fulfilled...How powerful is that? What if all our longings for our families, our businesses, our children, our health, and our nation were fulfilled? It is a tree of life to us when this happens. Our prayer should be: "Teach me how to pray, how to believe, how to walk in faith, and how to hope for better things in my life and in the lives of others."

"The tongue that brings healing is a tree of life, but a deceitful tongue crushes the spirit" (Prov. 15:4 NIV). So we pray, "Teach me how to talk, what to say, and how to say it. Help me understand how to refine my speech so it becomes a fountain of life to all who hear me. Let me hear words that bring healing and let me speak words that heal."

From Which Tree Will We Eat?

On the road to the tree of life are two decision pitfalls. One is lawlessness and the other is legalism. Lawlessness is our decision not to obey God but to live life our own way. Legalism is our decision to walk in the flesh and try to please God with works. Both lead to destruction.

Life says, "Christ is in me; it is Him I will live for, and it's His Spirit who will lead me." We open our spiritual ears to His wisdom and walk accordingly. James puts it like this:

> Who is wise and understanding among you? Let him show it by his good life, by deeds done in the humility that comes from wisdom. But if you harbor bitter envy and selfish ambition in your hearts, do not boast about it or deny the truth. Such "wisdom" does not come down from heaven but is earthly, unspiritual, of the devil. For where you have envy and selfish ambition, there you find disorder and every evil practice. But the wisdom that comes from heaven is first of all pure; then peace-loving, considerate, submissive, full of mercy and good fruit, impartial and sincere. Peacemakers who sow in peace raise a harvest of righteousness (James 3:13–18 NIV).

When you hear church members criticizing other churches, Christians comparing themselves to others, gossipers telling snippets of juicy details about someone, or pastors condemning and judging people, you will know where they've been eating their spiritual meals: at the tree of the knowledge of good and evil.

A survey of 3,348 people who left church revealed some amazing facts: 80 percent left as a result of conflict, gossip, and the lack of hospitality. That compares to only 18 percent who left because of a lack of solid Bible teaching.[1]

But when blessing and encouragement and instruction in righteousness precede people, how refreshing it is to believers and unbelievers alike. Where loving friendships endure and church members are open and hospitable to guests, you will find the life of God. When you see love permeating the church, you will know that life has entered its members' lives—and what a sweet life that is.

Now, ready for a sweet, juicy persimmon? Eat from the tree of life.

Staying in Life

As I write this chapter, I gaze out the window at my persimmon tree. I remember the fruit I ate from it last year. How delicious it was; I desire more. But the fact is, the American persimmon tree does not produce fruit every year. There is no fruit on this tree!

The truth is, it is difficult to eat only from the tree of life. It seems we run back and forth to whichever tree will benefit us at the moment. That is how the church gets its bad reputation: It is life-giving one week and then falls to the temptation of the tree of the knowledge of good and evil the next week. This happens in every church. But the church that can stay in life the longest wins...and wins big. Let that be our goal.

It happens to me and it happens to you. When things are going well, we are all about love and acceptance, forgiveness and hope. But just let someone cross us, and we swing like a threatened baboon from one tree to the other. Sad but true: Even as dedicated followers of Jesus, we still are partaking of good and evil at whim.

But thank God for our Advocate, Jesus Christ. First John 1:9–10 tells us, "If we confess our sins, he is faithful and just and will forgive us our sins and purify us from all unrighteousness. If we claim we have not sinned, we make him out to be a liar and his word has no place in our lives" (NIV).

Will life prevail? I think so. I have hope that more and more of our churches will remain in the tree of life so that we can grow in grace and in the knowledge of who we are in Him. As we reach up to the tree of life and partake of its fruit, it will be life-giving to us and we can share it with others. Healthy upreach creates attractional churches.

PART FOUR

The Ministry Philosophy of the Attractional Church

Chapter Fourteen

Doctrine, Interpretations, and Preferences

Even when all obvious barriers are removed, the wrong philosophy of ministry will inhibit growth. Most churches experiencing a plateau in growth need to change more than style and systems; they need a whole new life-giving philosophy for ministry. Without this change, nothing they do will bring consistent growth.

Philosophy is difficult to change because we are hard-wired with life experiences and belief systems that set our values and convictions. Many U.S. churches choose to ignore the success of attractional churches that are reaching underchurched people. As excuses, they say they are "holding on to [their] convictions."

I'd say they need to examine the convictions they're holding on to, check their biblical basis. Sometimes our values and convictions have their origin in family or even denominational tradition and not in Scripture.

Doctrine

Holding to the apostles' doctrine, that Christ came to fulfill the requirements of the law for salvation, is key to possessing a vibrant, growing church that can attract a city to Christ. A life-giving church is characterized by its gospel-centric orientation and the belief that the gospel of Jesus Christ, as the primary message of the Bible, cannot be compromised. This belief will not only produce conversion of the lost but give life to the unfulfilled. The Bible serves as the basic and continual instruction guide for the discipleship of believers.

Growing churches must adhere to nonnegotiable truths. These are truths we would die for. These are the ones that make us true followers of Christ. There are different degrees of emphasis put on subjects in the Bible, and leaders should reference those topics in the same balance that they appear in Scripture. However, we are often carried away by pet doctrines and run them into the ground. An example of this is physical healing. The fact that Christ heals is evident in Scripture. This has been testified by thousands and also in my personal life, therefore we preach healing. But if every time I get before a congregation all I talk about is healing, I would neglect other extremely important doctrines such as forgiveness, salvation, sanctification, and discipleship.

All doctrines are important, but some more than others. For example, some scholars catalog more than 162 references to hell in the New Testament alone, leading them to believe that hell is a major doctrine. There are only two major texts that address the role of women as teachers in church. Because of the difference in biblical emphasis, the doctrine of the role of women in the church is minor compared to the doctrine of hell. So, at the end of the day, we must admit that not all doctrines are equally important.

As many scholars say, there are narratives, and there are metanarratives. In other words, there are molehills and there are mountains. If we fail to stratify our emphasis on certain doctrines, we may very well spend our lives espousing the minor doctrines of the Bible while neglecting what really is important.

What we hold most dear is Scripture that leads us to salvation and instructs us in righteousness and true holiness. It is necessary, however, to know the difference between the fundamental doctrines of the Bible that we are willing to die for and personal interpretations. For example, your opinion on when Jesus is coming back is not as important as your opinion on whether Jesus is the Son of God. If He is not the Son of God, it doesn't matter if He comes back or not. Not all beliefs are equally important—but in some churches, you would never know the difference.

Interpretation of Scripture varies between churches and denominations. These differences are what cause groups to split and start their own brands of Christianity. Each values its position to the point that it builds an entire denomination around it.

We recognize that there are other interpretations of merit, ones other people will defend as fiercely as we defend ours. We qualify these positions with phrases such as "In my opinion," "The way I see it," or "I'm convinced of that." We would go so far as to say that these are our *convictions*. Though many well-meaning Christians and movements have parted over divergent interpretations, such interpretations are secondary in importance to the primary doctrines.

Some church groups and denominations elevate interpretations and traditional preferences to nonnegotiable truths. Pastor Greg Surratt calls it "conviction creep": when your interpretations or convictions creep onto your list of essential truths or nonnegotiable doctrines. Differences in interpretation have caused the emergence of religious factions, divisions, and splits over the centuries. It continues today.

There are nonnegotiable doctrines that make your church an authentic Christian community. There is clear teaching from Scripture on salvation and the person of Christ that we can never compromise. To violate these is to deny the fundamental teachings of the Bible and, in essence, to deny the faith. When we set aside truths in favor of pet doctrines—when we add our own opinions and man-made rules to Scripture—we move away from God's absolutes.

Among these nonnegotiable doctrines, some might add the sanctity of life and the return of Christ to gather up believers. Pentecostals and charismatics would add the baptism of the Holy Spirit and spiritual gifts. The Nazarenes, Anabaptists, Mennonites, and Wesleyans might add holiness as a second work of grace in the believer's life.

While there are some differences in these doctrines, for the most part each group would agree on the deity of Christ and His work on the cross. So, instead of looking at all the differences, let's compare what we have in common.

What Is Nonnegotiable?

The Lausanne Covenant (you can find it on the Web) is a statement of faith adopted by 2,300 evangelicals at the International Congress on World Evangelism in Lausanne, Switzerland. In 1974, 150 Christian leaders from around the world came to Lausanne to write an ecumenical confession, professing their shame for having failed to spread the gospel of Jesus. Billy Graham led the conference, and John Stott of England chaired the committee that drafted this document now adopted by a wide range of evangelicals. It focuses on what we all have in common and can agree on. These doctrinal positions are the nonnegotiable tenets of the Christian faith. I will call them *the gold standard* of beliefs, the distinguishable truths that make us followers of Christ.

No matter what creed or covenant we hold to that contains the nonnegotiable truths of our faith, everything else we believe falls into the categories of *interpretations* and *preferences*.

Interpretations

You may hear arguments about the interpretations of the Trinity or oneness of the Godhead, initial evidence of speaking in tongues when one receives the baptism of the Holy Spirit, different means of water baptism, the role of women in the church, tithing, divorce, and remarriage. Other doctrines that have been debated over the centuries that have caused many church divisions are:

- Eternal security vs. falling from grace
- Cessation of spiritual gifts vs. continuation of spiritual gifts
- Baptism of the Holy Spirit for empowerment vs. baptism of the Holy Spirit for salvation
- Election through predestination vs. election through foreknowledge
- Holiness as a second work of grace/divine holiness imparted vs. holiness as worked out in the believer's life by the believer

- Baptism of children vs. baptism of adults only
- Salvation at baptism vs. salvation as a profession of faith

No matter which position you take, you believe these interpretations with all your heart. In fact, you've probably had arguments over these interpretations with people you love. If you want to place a value on these beliefs, you might ask yourself: *Would I die for my stand on any of these doctrines?* Probably not. This is the litmus test that separates less-important doctrines from gold-standard beliefs. Therefore, to make them the primary message of your life, your church, your Sunday school class, or your small group would be to overemphasize one interpretation to the exclusion of others.

Preferences

Many churches adhere to traditional preferences. These positions are ingrained in us by exposure and experience. Historically, as people have tried to live out the Christian life they have made rules, which eventually formed codes of conduct and then became churches' standards. These deal mainly with style and rules of the local church and are often legalistic ideas about outward appearance and behavioral issues. They may even include the pastor's personal ideas of holiness and salvation. Preferences are more about *application* of doctrinal persuasion than about a truth itself.

Again, there is a tendency to elevate the application to the place of nonnegotiable truth. The end result is that adherence to these codes becomes the standard of belief more than the Scripture itself.

Hills We Will Die On

There are only a few nonnegotiable doctrinal "hills" that we should be willing to stake our lives on. For me, they are simple:

- Jesus is the one and only way to heaven.
- The cross of Christ is where Jesus shed His blood and paid for our sins.

- Faith in the work of Christ on the cross is the only means of salvation.
- There is only one God—the God of the Bible.
- The Bible is the full revelation and inerrant Word of God.
- There is a literal heaven and a literal hell.

Many other doctrines are eternally important to me. Many interpretations I hold dearly. And there are many Scriptures that people take to mean something different from what I believe they mean... and I will argue till the cows come home that my opinion is correct. But there are only a few hills that I am willing to die on.

The way you communicate a healthy philosophy of ministry to your church members is crucial. Most leaders adopt philosophies that will include one of these three categories of belief. One will stay with the gold standard of nonnegotiable truth, some will embrace interpretation, and others will go with preferences. Their beliefs profoundly affect their leadership style and, therefore, the attractability of their churches.

Chapter Fifteen

Leadership Styles

Never underestimate the influence of a leader. Whether positive or negative, your leadership style has as much to do with church growth as anything else. Your style affects your followers' morale, vision, and energy. It sets the tone, charts the direction, blazes new trails—or traipses aimlessly down the same old worn paths.

After working years in ministry, I have seen leaders fall into one of three leadership types: the Appreciator, the Navigator, and the Legislator. Some lend themselves to church growth—creating an attractional church—and some do not.

The Appreciator

This leader welcomes all outsiders with the love of God. Leaders at this level *appreciate*—they value, treasure, admire, and respect others.

An attitude of humility and a healthy fear of the Lord permeate every theological and methodological conversation. An Appreciator inspires an attitude of mutual respect: His church members can get along as long as Christ is exalted and the gospel is preached without compromise. The basic mission of Christ eclipses all else. The value of reaching souls reigns supreme, and petty arguments over doctrine and methodology take a backseat. The practical application of truth is more important than the minute details of doctrinal positions.

In his book *Natural Church Development,* Christian Schwarz writes, "Formal theological training has a negative correlation to both church growth and overall quality of churches."[1] Why? Is there anything wrong with theological training? Not necessarily. But many formally trained leaders preach from their ivory tower of knowledge and never connect with the heart of the person in the pew. Appreciator-leaders, on the other hand, speak to the felt needs of their communities with relevant messages that are biblically based and theologically sound.

In this environment, the leadership operates under the authority of Scripture, the Holy Spirit, and overseers. The pastor is driven by the love of God to reach people in all walks of life, and at all costs. These pastors accept all who come to hear the message. Acceptance does not mean "approval" but gives the church ample opportunities to share the gospel with the underchurched until they are converted to Christ and become productive members of the local church body.

The Great Commission inspires leaders to love all people and to reach out to nonbelievers around the world. The Appreciator-leader understands that people from different spiritual and social backgrounds will have varied opinions, values, and philosophies of life—and he is willing to love them for the opportunity to share Christ with them on a continuing basis. His church is generous and missions-oriented.

To hold the ministry together, the pastor and his staff depend on Spirit-led wisdom and Christ's love. The pastor helps members discover their gifts and, once identified, to use those gifts to serve in the church.

These leaders empower others to lead small groups and reach out to their city. The ministry is focused on Christ, the gospel, and serving.

The Appreciator has certain attributes that combine his gifting, style, and heart. Gifting helps the leader do what God has called him to do, and he employs a particular style to reach the lost, absent, and unfulfilled.

Attributes of the Appreciator-Leader

- Humility
- Acceptance
- Authenticity/transparency
- Preaches relevant messages
- Knowledgeable of Scripture
- Heart for the community
- Strategic in his plans
- Person of character/integrity/personal holiness
- Secure
- Focused on his mission
- Holy Spirit–led

The Appreciator's motive is to build the kingdom of God through reaching out to all people and bringing them into the life of the church through love and empowerment. He preaches a Christ-centered gospel and puts his resources into serving a lost community and equipping disciples to do the same.

If you possess some of these attributes, there is a good chance that your church is growing and reaching souls on a weekly basis. There is a good chance you have created an attractional church.

The Navigator

Navigator-leaders also preach the Bible but emphasize local or denominational interpretation. These are the things they have been taught to equate with scriptural absolutes but are really interpretations of Scripture. Their conclusions are debatable among members of the body of Christ. It's here that most denominations and churches split.

For example, John Calvin, a French theologian, was so strictly convinced that he was right about his doctrine of predestination that he condemned anyone who would disagree with him on major issues. In several cases where men disagreed with him, Calvin had them put to death for heresy. In fact, it is said of Calvin that he outlawed all sorts of crazy things that he deemed as "excessive" such as fishing, the color red, eating more than one type of meat in a single meal, even the height of a woman's hair.[2] (I can see the outlawing of some of these crazy things, but not fishing!)

The Navigator-leader thinks, *We are right and it is okay that others are wrong. We can get along as long as the others can be managed.* Leaders at this level navigate—they steer and direct their churches for the benefit of their own personal ministries.

In this model, the leader recognizes that in order to grow he must embrace a wider group of people, people who may not agree with him on everything. Therefore, he employs good management and political skills to increase the numbers who attend his church. He tolerates differences if doing so is good for him.

In most cases the church is driven by a capable communicator who collaborates with other like-minded church leaders. He is politically savvy and adept at managing his affairs and the affairs of the church. He employs team-management principles where a larger circle of influential people can have a voice.

This leader remains doctrinally sound, but again, he elevates interpretations to the level of nonnegotiable truths. Still, he listens to others without strongly resisting opposing views. Because he listens, he tries others' ideas and builds levels of leadership to carry out his well-managed plan. Everything has its place, the staff is well organized, programs are carried out consistently, and for the most part, financial matters are in order.

Because the leader is so proficient, he is very difficult to replace and his ministry is hard to reproduce. Usually these are founding pastors or men who have a long tenure as senior pastor. Their influence is so strong that it creates a kind of insecurity and intolerance toward diversity. In fact, according to the book *Breakout Churches* by Thom S. Rainer, the tenure of a senior leader has a certain impact upon a church's likelihood of growth.[3]

The Navigator has some of the qualities of an Appreciator-leader, but his emphasis is different. He is much more a strategist and manipulative for the sake of *his* ministry. He wants to reach people for Christ but is tolerant only when it benefits his cause. Castle builders build their own kingdoms; kingdom builders build the kingdom of God. This leader is a castle builder.

The Navigator presents a great public image, but for the most part, his private life is very much separate and...private. He does not come across as controlling to the congregation but is often intimidating to and overly demanding of his staff.

We were instructed in some of our schools of ministry not to get too close to the members of the church. We were told that if we did, we might lose our spiritual authority and not be able to lead them effectively. Navigator-leaders believe this. (And to think, Jesus walked with His disciples daily and lived among them every day.)

The Navigator allows no one other than himself to enjoy the limelight or credit. If an associate begins to excel and gets noticed, the Navigator-leader will confront him or pull him back. Because he knows the benefits of team ministry to his cause, he will allow certain loyal staff and followers to take an active part in his minis-try...with a short leash.

Attributes of the Navigator-Leader

- Good communicator
- Good knowledge of Scripture
- Politically savvy
- Seemingly tolerant of people who disagree with him
- Strategic
- Insecure—threatened by the success of others
- Private—puts on a false front publicly
- Territorial—doesn't like anyone or another church trespass-ing on his turf

The Navigator's motive is to build his personal kingdom by developing his image and managing those who come to be a part of his church. He preaches in order to reach people who will serve his best interests and personal agenda. He may have some fruit as a result, but all his effort is really about him.

The Legislator

I'm right and you're wrong: This is the attitude of the Legislator-leader. These leaders make laws and enforce them by intimidation and control.

This pastor's idea is that the only way for the church to be in unity is by everyone's agreeing with him on every single issue. In other words, the only way to true unity is uniformity. To protect themselves, the church members canonize all their opinions, thereby shutting down conversations that challenge their position. Concepts like questioning leaders and wrestling with doctrine are never seen as a means of learning; questioning is generally seen as subversive or rebellious. People learn through indoctrination. Much like building a wall around a medieval city, the barrier might protect the people within, but it also guarantees that others stay out unless they yield all control to the local leader.

In churches like this, the pastor is untouchable. The manipulative nature of these leaders creates a culture of distrust, confusion, anger, and loss of discernment. The drastic conclusion of Jim Jones's ministry in Guyana started with the Legislator-leader style. The leader's wrongdoing and suspicious behaviors are overlooked and even seem normal to followers. All financial matters are secretly held by one or two people in leadership, and no one is allowed to question them on any matter.

The fruit of this leadership is gossip, hate, narrow-mindedness, and intolerance in social and religious views. It creates blind followers who will not rise up for fear of being confronted by the pastor.

This kind of leadership is hardly ever reproducible; when the leader is gone, the church is left without direction. Very little is salvaged, including the followers' faith.

Another side effect of this mentality is that the church ignores the spiritual birth process. For example, a healthy baby takes nine months to grow in the womb before it's ready to be delivered. If you try to deliver a baby too soon, it's likely to experience defects and complications. Similarly, when sinners or new Christians are brought into this dysfunctional atmosphere, they are given very little time to deal with their issues or questions.

In effect, members in a Legislator-led church hint that they'll allow the new believer to swear, smoke, or wear immodest clothing for about a month. After that, he'd better conform, or else he threatens their standard of holiness. Rather than experiencing true transformation, after this amazingly short grace period the new believer hides sin and skepticism in the closet.

As a result, these churches are full of people who are secretly struggling with all sorts of questions and secret addictions. They must put up a false front just to be accepted in fear of retribution from the pastor or others in the church. They are trapped in a closed group and are too afraid or embarrassed to leave or to invite family and friends. Members are forbidden to question the leadership. Diversity and theological dialogue are simply too threatening to the unity and security of the group.

Concerns of the Legislator-Leader

- How you dress or beautify yourself for Sunday or any other day of the week
- Whether you are allowed to cut your hair
- Whether you should dance, watch TV, go to movies, or attend other social events
- What you should or should not eat and drink
- What kind of music the church plays or if it should play music at all
- Political persuasion as a doctrinal issue

Outward appearance and legalistic doctrines are the major themes of the sermons and the chatter at gossip parties. If this is what you hear and experience in your church, you have a Legislator-leader.

The preferences that are elevated to truth status are legalistically enforced all the way to the exclusion or excommunication of church members. And if you leave to go to another church, God forbid! The Legislator-leader will tell you that you might just end up in hell.

The Legislator-leader can be characterized as self-defined by his upbringing and personal views on Scripture and local church life. He lives by his own set of rules that reflect his personal weaknesses and temptations. He ignores the Great Commission and sometimes asserts that he and his followers are the only true Christians. He gathers a small flock that supports him financially, yet what he does could hardly be described as ministry. It is more the corralling of a few vulnerable souls into a fold he dominates with legalistic preaching. He can be very confrontational and critical of anyone who does not agree with his ideas.

The Legislator-leader focuses on the externals of life and demands outward perfection from his followers. His message is condemnation to the sinner and separation from the "world" to the congregation. Most of his sermons are shallow and deal with rules he thinks are important. Yet, because he is expert in certain doctrines, he comes across as a teacher of deep truths to a not-so-informed congregation. This type of leader does not need to worry about others taking credit for accomplishments—because there are none.

Attributes of the Legislator-Leader

- Leads from position, not influence
- Pressures everyone to give and to obey
- May know the Scriptures but preaches mainly from traditional preferences
- Insecure and very territorial; keeps others away from the flock
- Very legalistic; has biblical "proof" for every rule he wants to enforce
- Thinks she has the inside scoop on all truth, and that other churches and pastors are not spiritual
- Rarely releases anyone into ministry and holds on to people in his discipleship circle
- Likely to have many flaws that she covers up with a controlling, manipulative leadership style
- Always has an angle in his message and actions to manipulate his congregation to give a response that benefits him
- Insecurity motivates her actions; desires to be served, but unable to serve because of her own insecurity

The Legislator's motive is to get people to conform to his or her doctrine. He preaches conformity and is strict in his interpretation of Scripture. She wants her little flock to walk in obedience as she defines it.

Again, never underestimate the influence of a leader. If you want to create an attractional church, become and develop the kind of leader that draws believers and nonbelievers to your church: the Appreciator.

PART FIVE

Getting It Right

Chapter Sixteen

Twelve Characteristics of the Attractional Church

Think for a minute how you would answer this question: What do growing churches really do differently?

Now, think about your own church. If you have experienced seasons of growth, what were contributing factors for that growth? What about seasons of decline or stagnation—what figured in to driving people away from your church?

Could it be the environment in your church? Would you describe your church as attractional? Is it relevant, refreshing, and relational?

Does it offer life?

This chapter compiles all that you've read thus far, creating a sort of master list of characteristics of life-giving, healthy, and growing churches. (For purposes of definition, we identify a *growing church* as one engaged in vibrant ministry where souls are converted, thus increasing membership numbers.)

After having read through successful church scenarios in previous chapters, you may have a pretty good idea where your church is lagging. Or you may be confused as to what your church needs to grow.

Use this list to fine-tune your assessment. Prayerfully ask God to show you in which areas you need to work. Photocopy and distribute the survey in appendix C to get your church and ministry leaders' feedback on what is impeding your church's growth. What may be an appropriate course of action to nurture the areas in which you see a lack? In those areas of success, how do you maintain health and continue to grow?[1] I'll give you pointers for developing each of these attributes.

In his book, *Natural Church Development*, Christian Schwarz reveals the results of a study of over one thousand churches in the world where he discovers characteristics that contribute to church growth. With permission, I've added these characteristics to my list below.

1. Empowering Leadership

Leaders are openhanded. Leaders of attractional churches do not try to build up their own power to become all-powerful—exactly the opposite. One of their most important tasks is to help Christians develop greater degrees of empowerment, which, according to God's plan, already belongs to them.

- What are some biblical (and effective) ways to empower others?
- What are some specific ways in which you empower the members of your congregation?
- Do you lead from a posture of humility or position?

2. Gift-Oriented Ministry

God knows what your church is supposed to look like and sends people with the corresponding gifts to you. God has already determined which Christians should best assume which ministries in the church. The role of church leadership is to help its members identify their gifts and integrate them into ministries that match their gifts.

- What tools are in place to help members discover their gifts?

- Is your church adequately integrating members' various gifts into the church's ministries?
- Which members' gifts are going unnoticed or unused?
- Which ministries need gifts that belong to your members?

3. Passionate Spirituality

Your people love God. As far as healthy churches are concerned, studies show that the important thing (as long as spirituality is real) is not the way spirituality is expressed, but the fact that faith is actually lived out with commitment, fire, and enthusiasm.[2]

- How would you describe the way faith is lived out in your community—with devotion and joy? As drudgery or an obligation?
- How do your leadership and congregation view the connection between love for God and the way they "do" ministry?

4. Prayer and Fasting

Prayer was a daily act for the early church. Acts says, "They devoted themselves to the apostles' teaching and to the fellowship, to the breaking of bread and to prayer" (2:42 NIV) and "Everyday they continued to meet together in the temple courts" (Acts 2:46). We must ask God to help us become powerful in prayer. The disciples said to Jesus, "Lord, teach us to pray" (Luke 11:1 NIV). We should do the same.

Prayer and fasting are two of the most underutilized and misunderstood faith practices of the church. Develop a culture of prayer among your members and educate them on its importance and power. Make fasting a habit as a means of sacrificial praise, obedience, and trust (but urge your members to consult a doctor before undertaking any kind of fast). Lead your congregation in prayers of praise and petition. Good resources for prayer and fasting are C. Peter Wagner's book *Warfare Prayer* and Bill Bright's book *Seven Steps to Successful Fasting and Prayer*.

Prayer falls into two categories: fellowship with the Holy Spirit and spiritual warfare. Teach your members the differences between the two and lead by example as you pray in the different manners.

Most of our prayer time needs to be fellowship with the Holy Spirit: getting the mind of God, focusing on Him and listening for His voice, learning from His Word and thinking rightly about life issues. This is where God leads us to know Him and how He wants us to live in the world. We learn from Him and get directions for our lives and find peace in His presence.

In spiritual warfare, you confront the schemes of the enemy. First build yourself up in the Lord by focusing on Him; this allows you to gain the spiritual strength to take on the enemy. Once you are filled with power through worship and God-focused prayer, then you are ready to pray offensively against the contrary powers.

- What is your understanding of prayer and fasting?
- What is your congregation's understanding of prayer and fasting?
- How do you discover prayer needs among your congregation?
- How does God answer prayer?
- How does God respond to fasting?

5. Compassionate, Need-Oriented Evangelism and Missions

Demonstrating compassion for hurting people is as close to the heart of Christ as you can get. When a culture of compassion for the needy permeates the local church, the light of God will shine in their hearts. Jesus' passion was and is to relieve the pain of people who suffer.

The attitude toward world missions in a local church is so powerful that it can shape the worldview of members as effectively as anything else we do. When the culture of the church embraces the world as its field of labor, the boundaries of personal involvement enlarge. World missions are a huge part of creating a God-centered culture in an attractional church.

Praying for the lost, giving to missions, and celebrating changed lives create a culture that makes others the reason we exist. Connecting to the disconnected becomes the passion of the church.

- How do non-Christians view your church and its ministries?
- How do you evangelize the lost?
- How would you describe your church's passion (or the lack thereof) for evangelism?
- How is your church engaged in world missions?
- Would you describe your church culture as more self-centered or others-centered? Why?

6. Endurance, Tenacity, and Perseverance

I know too many people who walk away from the church and Christ whenever they encounter hardships. But endurance is the sign of a good soldier and the mark of a true follower of Christ, according to 2 Timothy, "Endure hardness with us like a good soldier of Jesus Christ" (2:3 NIV).

During the days of the "rescue" movement at abortion clinics—when many Christians protested the abortion deaths of unborn children—our church in Baton Rouge was involved. One morning at daylight, hundreds of Christians gathered to march outside a clinic that was performing abortions. Men and women of every age and race walked arm in arm. I watched them take abuse from supporters of the radical Right to Choice groups and a certain group of penitentiary guards who were brought in. Many protesters were injured and some were sent to hospitals, but they were not deterred. This event was politically charged and the rescue movement was heavily criticized.

But I was proud of what I saw: These Christians were willing to suffer for what they believed in their hearts was the cause of Christ on behalf of the unborn.

There's something about suffering together that breeds solidarity and creates strength. Whether it's fighting for a common cause or getting dirty during a church workday, persevering through times of hardship, transition, and difficulty makes your church grow heartier.

- How has your church suffered, and how did members respond during that time?
- What blessings have you witnessed from others' perseverance through suffering?
- How do you encourage perseverance among your members? Among the church leaders?

7. Functional Structures, Location, and Logistical Arrangements

Does it work? Is it obvious, easy, and strategic? Church structures are never an end in themselves but only a means to an end. The most important criterion for forms and structures in the church is that they fulfill their purpose. Healthy churches change (or lay to rest) whatever does not measure up to this requirement.

Consider all that goes under the facilities and logistics heading: buildings, parking lot, restrooms, seating, audio, heating/air-conditioning, signs, advertising, greeting visitors, ushers, and so on. You can ascertain much about how your church is doing in this area with one crucial question: Does each of these things work?

My friend Cory Hardesty drove to visit a new church. When he pulled into the parking lot, there was no one outside. The place looked a little scary from the parking lot, and because he did not know what to expect on the other side of the front door, he and his family just drove away. This particular church's method of greeting people did not work.

Cory skipped church that day because of the unknowns about that church and its people. He didn't want to just walk into a strange place without some introduction or welcome. From the outside, the church looked unfriendly and cold.

On the other hand, if there had been friendly and welcoming people, especially his age, showing them where to take their children and introducing them to others, surely Cory and his family would have gone in. An environment of acceptance would have opened Cory's heart to attend. For an underchurched person, the right environment would open his heart not only to attend but to hear and accept the Word.

Creating a safe environment for the lost, absent, and unfulfilled starts before anyone steps inside the church building. The way we market our churches creates perception. This involves presenting clear directions to the church on our website, greeting people in the parking lot and in the sanctuary, and speaking to them in our services. It's how the restrooms are maintained, if visitors can find the children's classes easily, whether the service begins on time, and whether the messages are relevant.

It all matters and it all has an impact.

- Make a comprehensive list of all the aspects of the logistics of your church—from the website to visitor follow-up. How can you improve in any of these areas? What impact do you think these improvements will have on the growth of your church?
- How is your building/space/campus working for you?
- How does your church attract and treat visitors?

8. Inspiring Worship

The most important question about the worship service is whether it is an inspiring experience for those who attend. People who attend inspiring worship services unanimously declare that the church service is—and for some Christians this is almost a heretical word—*fun*.

Many pastors not only miss the application of God's Word as it relates to everyday life, but they also often preach bad news instead of good news. Pastors seem to get stuck on the consequences of sin instead of the benefits of the Cross. They focus on the consequences of unbelief and not the joys of surrender to Christ. Some pastors need surgery...a "Pharisee-ectomy"!

Giving messages that condemn and accuse people zaps life

from the believer and hope from the lost. This is the method pastors of failing churches use week after week. It's no wonder that a high percentage of U.S. churches are declining or have reached a plateau.[3]

Messages of good news that can be readily applied to real-life situations and that come from love, not condemnation, give life. Once we get a deeper revelation of grace we will depart from legalism.

Once again, the early church in Acts gives us a helpful model of what it means to give clear messages that offer inspired worship. With the Old Testament as their backdrop of truth, the apostles preached the good news of the kingdom of God. Their message: *Jesus has come to fulfill all that the Law and Prophets spoke of.* The message was as pure as it was simple: *Humankind is in sin, hopeless, and lost. Christ has come to save us all from our sin. The sacrifice of Jesus Christ on the cross is payment for the sin of all humankind.* The doctrine of the Cross is the big idea. The preaching of the Cross is the prevailing message. *Believe!* How simple is that?

Peter preached on the day of Pentecost, saying,

> Each of you must repent of your sins, turn to God, and be baptized in the name of Jesus Christ to show that you have received forgiveness for your sins. Then you will receive the gift of the Holy Spirit. This promise is to you, and to your children, and even to the Gentiles—all who have been called by the Lord our God. . . . Save yourselves from this crooked generation! (Acts 2:38–40 NLT).

This is the answer to the Law and the Prophets that Jesus spoke about. This is the kingdom of God message.

One can only imagine how excited the Jews were when, having been under the Law for generations, they heard about God's grace. There were outbursts of joy and praising God in the streets of Jerusalem. This contagious exuberance spread throughout the entire known world fueled by one thing: the apostles' doctrine, the message of Jesus Christ.

- What's worship at your church like—fun? Inspiring? Thought-provoking? Boring? Stale?
- How would you describe the messages of your church? Are those messages fueled by the apostles' doctrine?
- What is the response to Sunday morning worship? If it's not life-changing joy and praise, why not?

9. Holistic Small Groups

Many healthy churches have developed a system of small groups where individual Christians can find intimate community, practical help, and intensive spiritual interaction. These groups become the essence of the true life of the church as participants apply biblical insight to the everyday issues of the participants.

Sunday services cannot provide the discipleship that small groups can. The more intimate setting allows new believers to grow comfortably in relationship with other Christians. These relationships provide mentoring and provide examples for the new members to follow. New believers receive instruction, learn biblical application to life issues, and establish accountability partners while in small groups. These groups are indispensable in creating culture in the local church.

- How do small groups function in your church?
- What further benefits could your small-group ministry offer your church members?

10. Giving and Sharing

As we learn to give to the church and share with others, we tap into the goodness of God and His provision. It is through generosity that we learn the heart of God. A giving culture is an expression of the nature of God.

Sharing is a huge part of fellowship in the New Testament. Acts 2:42, 44 says that the believers ate meals together, and in fact they shared everything they had. It cost the new believers something to claim Christ. "Everything they had" might not be much by today's standards but it was truly "everything they had" back then.

The spirit of these Scriptures fires me up. I know that few of us today are willing to share everything we have with new believers, and as a result we feel a little convicted when we read these words. But if we would be willing to share some of what we have on a consistent basis to provide for new Christians a place of worship, fellowship, and care, we would recapture that spirit of generosity.

Let your faith cost you something. Let evangelism, discipleship, leadership training, and fellowship cost you something personally, and you will share in the joy of the salvation of new believers. I believe it is necessary for us not only to tithe but to personally take on the expense of bringing up new believers as disciples. Then we will know what biblical sharing is all about.

Like most people, I don't throw my money around every time I am asked to give. But the harvest and discipleship of new believers are things that I need to not only invest in but to sacrifice for. It is in this spirit of generosity and giving that the early church became so well known and accepted by masses of everyday people. It fueled the evangelistic efforts of the church, and "each day the Lord added to their fellowship those who were being saved" (Acts 2:47 NLT).

Selling Out

Christians in Jerusalem sold everything they had and divided their possessions for the very practical purpose of feeding and caring for all those who were in Jerusalem for Pentecost. Acts 2:45 says they "sold their possessions and goods, and divided them among all, as anyone had need" (NKJV). Who exactly shared in this unprecedented act of benevolence? "All who believed were together, and had all things in common" (v. 44 NKJV). They didn't distribute the proceeds to unbelievers but to other believers who stayed in Jerusalem after Pentecost.

The new followers of Christ didn't have Visa or American Express cards, so they took what they had, sold it, and used the cash to buy food and other provisions. They shared their own clothes, dishes, and everything else. They were poor compared to today's Western standards, yet they liquidated their meager possessions to meet the needs of people who were being saved.

We are worlds apart from the Day of Pentecost event in Jerusalem, but we can learn a lot from it. The environment on the first day of the early church cannot be compared to the church twenty-one hundred years later, but we can see the total commitment of the early church to the evangelization of the lost and their willingness to invest their earthly possessions to care for those who came to Christ. We should do the same.

Firewood and Watermelons

In the early 1980s, during the Carter administration, when inflation and interest rates went through the ceiling, some local industries began to lay off workers and even close their doors. Money was tight as Federal Reserve Chief Paul Volcker cut the money supply and brought the United States into a "forced" recession. At the time I was the pastor of a small church in West Monroe, Louisiana. Most of my congregation members were in construction or worked at one of the paper mills in town. Several also worked for the General Motors Guide Lamp plant. When the General Motors plant closed and one of the paper mills went out of business, thousands were left unemployed. The end result was that nearly 30 percent of my congregation was without an income. It was a tough time in the life of our church, but it worked to our good.

During the hard times of the recession, the church was often in danger of not having enough money to pay the monthly church note. I remember how I struggled with the thought of not being able to honor our word with the bank. But instead of just riding it out, we worked together and never missed a single note while I was pastor. Several weekends, the men and I would cut firewood and go around town selling it at homes where we saw fireplaces. My associate pastor, Darrell Griggs, even sold watermelons from his personal patch one summer to help meet the bills. During the hardest of these times I actually gave up my salary and started my own business until the economic tide changed.

We did what had to be done. We practiced accountability and

stewardship. We grew in numbers during those years and never missed our commitments to our debtors or our missionaries. We were an attractional church with a huge vision for missions. We fulfilled our role even in the hardest of times. We shared our resources for the cause of Christ.

- How would you describe your church's attitude toward its resources?
- How do your church members sacrifice for and invest in one another and new believers?
- What is the biggest challenge in encouraging generosity among your members? What steps will you take to overcome this challenge?

11. Establishing and Maintaining Loving Relationships

Healthy churches manifest a measurably higher "love quotient" than do stagnant or declining churches. Unfeigned, practical love endows a church with a much greater magnetic power than all the marketing efforts of this world.

David Kinnaman of the Barna Group reports that unchurched people often have the perception that if they go to a church for help, they will be judged.[4] Jesus says in John 13:34–35, "Love one another. By this all men will know that you are my disciples, if you love one another" (NIV). Jesus didn't say, "Because of your perfect theology or your extreme judgment of sin, all men will know that you are my disciples."

Our zeal for loving our community is the transforming ingredient.

The culture of love does not judge; rather, it believes the best of people, and it seeks the best for people. It is a tall order to walk consistently in love for others, especially when they do wrong, but love doesn't take wrongdoing into account, according to 1 Corinthians 13:5.

Most important, love never fails. In Matthew 22:36–39 Jesus was asked, "Teacher, which is the greatest commandment in the Law?"

Jesus said, "'Love the Lord your God with all your heart and with all your soul and with all your mind.' This is the first and greatest commandment. And the second is like it: 'Love your neighbor as yourself'" (NIV).

How great is love in your church? Look at the commandment to love God with all your heart and soul and mind: There must be love first of all.

Forgiveness

Don't make the mistake of looking at forgiveness in a clinical way. If we try to examine forgiveness in the light of the Law (who was right and who was wrong), we will miss the spirit of forgiveness. We are called upon by God to forgive often and fully just as He forgives us often and fully. The Scripture is clear about this, but we have difficulty fleshing it out because it goes against the grain of our human nature. Forgiveness is not natural; it is supernatural. So we need God's grace working in us in order to forgive.

Forgiveness is absolutely necessary for walking in good favor with God. We read in Mark, "When you stand praying, if you hold anything against anyone, forgive him, so that your Father in heaven may forgive you your sins" (Mark 11:25 NIV). We need the Father to forgive our sins; therefore, we must forgive. It is that simple.

We have all been offended by people we love and by those we love little or not at all. Often when this happens it takes a long time for us to release them from the offense. At the least it changes the way we approach these offenders, think of them, or let them back into our lives. When we forgive them, forgiveness accomplishes two things immediately that are huge benefits to us personally. First, the pressure is taken off the relationship. We are freed to look at them in an innocent way with no animosity. Second, we are freed from the control that unforgiveness has over our lives.

How can being unforgiving control us? We all respond to situations in a manner that reflects how we feel about the people involved. We won't go to a Christmas party if that particular person is there. We avoid him or her at church or go to another church if the offending party attends. We allow the offense to control our emotions for years and are under the cloud of the offense until we forgive.

Something like this came to surface at a church I know well. It was the church I started in 1976. Here's the story.

One of my daughters had a friend come over to spend the night. For fun they started making prank phone calls. As providence would have it, I caught them. I had a long talk with the girls, sent the friend home, and punished my daughter. After that event I refused to let my daughter hang out with this girl. This wasn't the girl's fault; it was my daughter's fault. I just felt that if my girl felt comfortable doing things like this with her friend, maybe it would be best that they didn't hang out together. I always liked this friend of my daughter and always spoke highly of her. It was just a parental decision to step in and stop the relationship. The parents of the girl were upset with me, but it was my call and I stuck by it.

What I did not realize was that my decision to sever the relationship between my daughter and this friend of hers would cause long-term pain and distress to her and her family. Was my choice to separate the relationship too harsh of a punishment? Was there a less extreme measure that I could have taken? I discovered the answer to this many years later.

Twenty-seven years later, when I preached at this church again, the mother of this girl asked if she could speak with me. Her opening words took me by complete surprise: "Brother Billy, you just don't know how much pain and heartache you have caused my family."

I responded, "What are you talking about?"

She recounted the story that I just told and said that her daughter and her family have suffered all these years because of the rejection that they felt from my not allowing her daughter to be my girl's friend. I couldn't believe that she had harbored these feelings for twenty-seven years, but she had. Those unforgiving feelings had robbed her of joy and of personal forgiveness. Perhaps my failure to handle the situation in a more moderate way and allow the girls to remain friends was the catalyst for the pain that they had gone through. It was obvious that bitterness had taken root and had controlled her for nearly three decades.

My wife and I love this family, and I did what I could to console her and let her know that I never held anything against her precious daughter. I am not sure it did any good. Forgiveness would have been the best route for both of us to take.

- What's your church's "love quotient"?
- How could that increase among your congregation?
- How would a visiting non-Christian feel—loved or condemned—among the members of your church?
- How forgiving is your congregation? Do you know of any people holding grudges against each other?
- When have you seen unloving and unforgiving forces at work and what destruction did they cause? What could have been done to nip that in the bud?

12. Bible-Based Foundation

Without this attribute, your church is just another social club. Sure, the first eleven are key components of an attractional church, but this one is the absolute source of life-giving nourishment.

The church must preach and teach from the Bible. The most relevant, refreshing, and relational aspect of the church is the good news of Christ. It should go without saying that to sacrifice the truth of the message of the Word of God for any of the aforementioned characteristics not only halts church growth, it is also an egregious error.

Remain faithfully committed to the Word of God as you simultaneously seek to grow your church.

- How does your church stay true to the Bible?
- If there are any areas of creeping error among members, what needs to be done to steer your church back to scriptural truths?
- Realize that personal "revelations" and strange deductions from Scripture that beat a fine but crooked line through Scripture must eventually be rejected by informed believers.

Life-Giving or Life-Taking?

Have you ever left a church service and felt as if the very life had just been sucked out of you? The people, the service, and the pastor left you feeling confused, condemned, and worthless. Or it was so boring that you felt exhausted both physically and mentally. Yes, you just experienced a life-taking church service, the kind that you find often in churches across the United States.

It doesn't have to be this way. We've seen what John 10:10 tells us: "I came so they can have real and eternal life, more and better life than they ever dreamed of" (The Message).

Churches should be a fresh expression of the life of Christ, loving God, loving others, and loving life. This is church twenty-first-century style, where people share Christ naturally and effectively, exercise areas of gifting and passion, and grow personally, professionally, and spiritually.

The attractional church gives life. It's relevant, refreshing, and relational.

Chapter Seventeen

Doing It Right but Not Growing?

In your journey as a pastor, becoming self-aware may well be one of your greatest acts of courage. I hate to say it, but if you think you're doing everything right but you're still not growing, the truth is you're probably not doing everything right. The good news is that if you are even asking the title question of this chapter, you're in a good place. At least you know you're not achieving your maximum possible impact for the kingdom of God and you've created an opportunity for courage, change, and growth!

The key to growth and impact is change...Change something, change something major, and change something now. The world changes, and we must change to meet the world where it evolves. Nearly nothing is the same as it was ten years ago, and it will be different five years from now. Like the old adage says, if you do what you've always done, you'll get what you've always got. To create a life-giving, attractional church from a stagnant one, here's another adage: Wisdom is knowing what to change, knowledge is knowing how to change, and courage is being willing to change.

To experience new growth and vitality in your church, you must transform your approach to ministry. My brother, friend, and fellow minister Scott Hornsby has demonstrated the concepts of this chapter as well as anyone I know.

Case Study: Fellowship Church Zachary

Nothing is more frustrating and tiring than to hold services week after week and never see growth in your church. You begin to doubt your call into the ministry and even your salvation at times. You begin to hate the ministry, and your mind wanders off to hobbies or other interests. You've done everything you know to do and it's just not happening.

Is this you? If so, read on. You are not alone.

Scott has been a pastor for more than twenty-five years. For nearly twenty years, Scott's church fluctuated up and down, along with the starts and stops in the population of the town it was in. For the most part, the church was stuck on a plateau of around one hundred members—one hundred good-hearted, fervent, God-fearing people.

Sundays at his church were a big event. Everyone came to church fashionably late and definitely in fashion. My brother would dress to the nines in his good-looking Sunday suit, ready to *bring the heat*! The music was always lively but not near as lively as the people. Every service was a mix of classic old-time songs and a southern Louisiana brand of music referred to as "Bayou Gospel Boogie." And nearly every service would have at least a few people dancing in the Spirit, a prophetic word, an offering sermon, or worship "soaking time," a time where people linger at the altar to get God's blessing. After about forty-five minutes of ministry, Scott would begin to preach.

And my brother could preach. He'd start up in cruise control, but before you knew it, he'd be screaming (literally) like a Harley-Davidson. And he got plenty of help from the congregation. Soon there'd be hanky waving and shouting and clapping. On a good day, Scott would speak for at least ninety minutes, depending on the Spirit's leading (and the New Orleans Saints football schedule).

His services were full-blown charismatic gospel meetings. They were intense and often just too much for the average visitor to handle. Visitors would come once but almost never twice. Scott was caught in the trap of having services that pleased a small group of people who ignored the necessary changes that would reach the underchurched.

Despite all the fervor and good intention, the revival meetings, and even the special guest speakers, Scott's church membership still hovered at one hundred people. It seemed that was the limit.

One day, after some courageous prayer, reflection, and self-analysis, Scott decided it was time to make some serious changes. Now, five years later, Scott's church has an average of eight hundred in weekly attendance. It flourishes with new people and new life. In fact, this past Easter, Scott's church had 1,250 people in attendance, and more than 125 decisions were made for Christ. The changes have been a revelation for him and for the city he is trying to reach for Jesus.

The changes he made, you can make too.

Admit There's a Problem

For Scott, it wasn't easy and it wasn't quick. He had to first admit that the way he was doing church was not effective. Then he had to start changing everything that held him back from seeing the fruit he so desperately desired. So he started with himself. He changed his attitude and opened himself up to mentors who could lead him. He had to exchange the shout for the harvest.

Fellowship Church Zachary is in a small suburb of Baton Rouge and is one of the best examples of a successful transition from a traditional model of church to a life-giving attractional model. The transition was made incrementally and consistently. The results have been amazing.

Change is the prerequisite of improvement. Before you can improve, you have to make the correct changes. In order to have continuous improvement, you have to be committed to continuous change...not changing everything, but changing what needs to be better or different. First, you have to admit something needs change.

Rethink Time

Time is the greatest commodity of the twenty-first century. People cherish what little time they have on the weekends, and they avoid anything that seems to waste time unless it is very entertaining. Scott's services were too long. Many times they would last for two hours or more. It was difficult for his members to sit through long worship sets and even longer sermons. Visitors were totally exhausted when they left, their kids were hungry and crying, and it was counterproductive.

The first change Scott made was to rethink timing. To begin with, Sunday services were limited to no more than one hour and fifteen minutes. That's right, seventy-five minutes max. To his surprise, no one complained about shorter services.

Starting on time is also an important component. The tendency is to wait for people to get to church...so you delay just a little getting started. You begin to start later and later and people get the message that there is no reason to come on time. You are in a catch-22. The later you start, the later they come. Just start on time every time and don't wait for people to get there.

Adjust Your Preaching Style

The next thing Scott changed was his style of preaching. Scott was a screamer. I used to be a screamer. I wanted to make sure that the saints stayed awake and that the sinners heard me! That might have worked back in the day but not anymore. Scott began to tone down his preaching to more conversational levels. With shorter talks, more civil tones, and less rabbit chasing, his messages became more informative, relevant, and enjoyable. People began to comment how much the messages helped them and started bringing friends and family to church, confident they wouldn't be embarrassed by a browbeating sermon. Things started turning around.

Less Legalism and Fewer Gimmicks

Shorter services and more civil tones in Scott's talks gave him a greater audience. The next thing that began to disappear was the legalism. Instead of walking out of church feeling condemned and embarrassed, people found hope in a message of acceptance, forgiveness, and grace. They learned that God wasn't mad at them but wanted to rescue them from the consequences of sin and rid them of the shame associated with it. This was huge. People were liberated from guilt and condemnation and their love for God soared. And as the messages became more relevant, people started commenting how church met needs in their lives.

Then there were the altar calls. Before the transition, there were long altar calls where people came forward for prayer where all kinds of emotional manifestations took place, such as falling down on the floor, shouting, and shaking. It might have been fun and even refreshing for regulars, but visitors couldn't wait to get out of the building. Now, Scott asks for a simple response to accept Christ and gives everyone an opportunity to receive prayer after the service is over, as people are exiting the building.

Creativity and Advertising

Then there was creativity. As the church began to change, the leaders employed creative components that made it more interesting and effective. Video roll-ins, props, meaningful music, and stories related to the messages were produced weekly by the staff. All the creative efforts just made the services more interesting and relevant. Scott began to make the Bible more clear and applicable to daily life.

Once you get your ministry to an effective place, it's time to advertise. Get the word out about your church, your new sermon series, and the outreaches you will be involved in. Let people know you are there on a regular basis. Use all the social media available and get the members involved. It has never been as easy to get your message out as it is today. Twitter, Facebook, and your website are tools you should use every day. Then use mail-outs and other means of advertizing at least twice a year to blanket your city with news about your church. You can never stop advertising.

Scott used the local community newspaper to advertise his services and all upcoming events, allowed school board meetings and city meetings to be held in his church, and also sponsored the track team for their local high school. Each of these turned out to be huge advertising wins for his church.

One more thought: Even with the best media advertising and social media, word of mouth is still the best form of marketing. But with word of mouth, you don't determine when it happens; your people do. Once you transition to a more interesting and effective Sunday service, people will tell others and invite them to come. When this begins to happen you will grow...and grow. If your members like everything you do, they will invite everyone they know.

Steward Visitors Well

People will come to a service where they are allowed to remain anonymous. They will be attentive and comfortable. The right approach to visitors will create this feeling of safety. This is exactly what happened with Scott.

He discovered that the best way to create this safe environment is to allow people to make the first move in letting you know they are coming. When they fill out a visitor's card, attend a newcomers' meeting, or join a small group, they are saying, "Okay, I'm here!"

Never ask visitors to identify themselves or trick them into revealing who they are—they might feel manipulated. Rather, just thank visitors for coming as part of your opening statements and let them enjoy the service. If you give them a safe and life-giving experience, they will be back, and you will find out who they are soon enough.

At Seacoast Church in Charleston, South Carolina, the church has a monthly staff meeting where we heard pastor Greg Surratt's heart and vision for the church. We also read postcards that visitors sent in about what they had experienced at one of our services. We asked three simple questions and most of the answers we received were right on point as to what we needed to change. Here are the questions:

1. What did you notice first?
2. What did you like best?
3. What could we improve on?

After visitors filled out the cards, they dropped them in the offering box. First Touch ministry would take the cards and send letters thanking the visitors for attending and enclosed the three questions on a self-addressed, postage-paid postcard. It was easy for them to fill out the postcards and put them in the mailbox. Many attractional churches have their own versions of the same concept, done in different ways. We call these "connection cards."

One thing Greg Surratt at Seacoast does to get more people to fill out the card is to give them a hassle-free guarantee. This is a promise not to call them, stop by, or attempt in any way to contact them. If the visitors want to have the church contact them, they have to initiate it. Greg's staff let visitors know this up front, and this has increased the number of people who fill out the cards by 300 percent. With the feedback from the cards, each department can make necessary adjustments to their ministry.

Responses like "We had a difficult time finding the nursery" or "We had to park too far away from the building" revealed vital information for improving what Seacoast offered its visitors. Whatever the responses on the cards, the staff acted on it. Every month issues were being addressed and action was being taken to make church better.

And better it got. Getting this kind of feedback is the best way to start.

Steward Finances Well

One of the biggest complaints people have about churches is feeling as if the pastor just wants their money. In some cases that perception is justified. When you hear pastors go on and on about how God will bless you if you give your tithe or offering, you get the impression the church will go under if you don't give. Then there is the five- to fifteen-minute offering teaching. All this does is reinforce in the minds of people that you really do just want their money. This makes the service longer and gives visitors a reason not to come back.

The offering should be part of the service. After all, giving is a biblical principle that honors God. But don't make giving a business transaction—instead, make it an act of worship. That's what Scott did. People don't want to feel that they owe the church money and are therefore taking part in a business transaction. They want to feel as if they are worshipping God with their giving and that He will honor them for it.

Stewardship begins at the church office. When the church handles its finances wisely and gives generously to the community, people will give more liberally. But if you mishandle the monies and are always begging from the pulpit, people will respond by tightening their purse strings. No one likes to fund poor stewardship.

Invest in a Consultant

First impressions, worship style, and message content and relevancy are all important pieces of the successful church puzzle, and I have covered them in other parts of this book. It may be, however, that you need someone with fresh eyes to come to your church to give you an accurate appraisal of your ministry. A good consultant can help you get to where you want to go faster than almost anything else. Scott asked a friend from another church to attend his services and give him weekly critiques; he also spoke with pastors of other churches who were having successful ministries. Many consultants come as "secret shoppers" and can give helpful critiques.

Scott was very courageous to transition Fellowship Church into a life-giving church. It took determination, persistence, and guts... and he prevailed in a big way. The church seems like a totally different place. Souls are being added weekly, income is climbing, and people bring guests every week. The people love the life-giving environment and actually enjoy church.

Make sure your church is offering essential services, creating a welcoming atmosphere, and keeping a close eye on ways to improve.

Change is in the air...embrace it!

Chapter Eighteen

A Wonderful Future for Your Church

Families are not perfect because people aren't perfect; the same is true for the church you lead. But no matter how imperfect or even dysfunctional your church is, it can be the place people can turn to with the troubles in their lives.

My colleague, Guy Walker, saw his first church unravel. Once Guy moved from a troubled church to Church of the Highlands, he realized there were churches that could actually help him deal with his issues and equip him to help others deal with theirs. It was a different kind of church with leaders who were secure and reached out to him and his friends out of the love of God. He says, "Under this kind of leadership at Highlands, I was able to move from superficial, self-reliant attitudes to a total trust that God was working in me to further His kingdom."

Think about it. Jesus is the Head of God's church, and the church will overcome the world. When you hear people talking about the failure of the church, know that they are speaking of a local and limited situation. For every struggling church, God is raising up a dynamic life-giving church to take its place. That is why I believe there is a great future for the local church in America.

Why Your Church Has a Great Future

God Cares

Jesus said, "The gates of hell shall not prevail against [the church]" (Matthew 16:18 KJV). No matter what critics say about the local church, we have God's guarantee that He will do what is necessary to cause the body of Christ to overcome. We have His power, His Spirit, and His people at work in the church to give us ultimate success.

Life Is Back

The modern movement toward the attractional model has changed the landscape from declining churches to powerful, fast-growing churches. These dynamic churches will eventually overcome the decline of church attendance in the United States and create a surge in attendance in the years to come.

America Wants a Church with Life

Most Americans want to see a strong, vibrant church even if their current experience is negative. Once people realize that church can meet their needs, they will rush to reconnect. When they find life and a meaningful spiritual climate, they will begin to bring others along.

Denominations Desire Growth

Many denominations and movements are making adjustments in their philosophy in order to reach others. They are looking outside denominational walls to find training and coaching that will allow them to turn their organizations around.

People Need Hope

People need hope, and the local church is the hope of the world. Attractional churches have discovered a way to bring hope back to their communities through relevant and accepting ministries that speak authentically to the needs of hurting people.

Generally, even with the decline of the church, many Americans are concerned that the church needs to regain its place of importance and prominence in our country. Eighty percent still identify themselves as Christians even though they may not go to church, and 70 percent say they are committed to Jesus. Sixty percent say they are churched.[1]

This tells me that a majority of people in the United States want to be part of the church of Jesus Christ; they're simply waiting for the local church to take the lead.

Leaders Are Ready

With the resurgence of small groups and empowered leaders, the ministry of the church now relies on grassroots growth more than ever. An effective means of shepherding the flock is through members who are highly trained to serve as small-group leaders. In terms of human resources and cost, small groups are the efficient way to reach our cities for Christ.

God is at work to reestablish His church in the United States regardless of how it may have failed in the past. We need to prepare our hearts and minds to accept the fact that the church is coming back in a prevailing way. There is an awakening coming; all the signs are present. If we will get ready, God will use us to lead a spiritual breakthrough for our nation.

The Signs of Revival

Here are a few signs of awakening I see in America today.[2]

First, awakenings always emerge against a backdrop of serious spiritual decline or intense spiritual dryness. The statistics in chapter 1 point to decline and alarm about the church's ineffectiveness. The strong contrast between the conservative and liberal churches is getting even more distinct. Social trends are making deep lines of demarcation deeper as the liberal denominations are getting still more liberal. The conservative churches are learning to be more accepting but realize that approval of sinful lifestyles can't be their message. They are depending more on the power of God to bring deliverance to people who are in bondage to vices and lifestyles that the Bible condemns.

Second, awakenings are the product of intense prayer. When people pray for revival, God seems to answer their prayers in ways they least expect. At the beginning of an awakening, people often feel an exhilarating sense of expectancy. In our country, prayer is on the front burner for many of the new prevailing churches. Where churches are praying and fasting, we are seeing many come to Christ for the first time and others healed and set free.

At a specific point in the outset of an outpouring of the Holy Spirit, God's presence is suddenly recognized. The power of God falls spontaneously and continuously. I don't mean small pockets of isolated events that all the spiritual zealots run to see. Their enthusiasm takes them to any city where so-called signs and wonders are reported and they immediately buy into the "revival." Nearly 100 percent of the time, these things fizzle out prematurely.

Real revival is characterized by a sustainable stream of souls turning to Christ. It is an awakening to the reality of God that renews the faith of an entire nation. Communities are transformed by the power of God working through local ministries. Awakenings of this kind seem to emerge at the same time in many different places.

Who becomes involved? The Lord breathes new life into the church. Not just a church, but His church universally. He brings multitudes of new believers into His body in all denominations and movements. Backsliders are reclaimed, and people often come out of curiosity or skepticism and become believers.

The spread of the news usually takes place by word of mouth. There is normally not only intentionality on the part of new converts but intense strategy and prayer by local churches to produce a book-of-Acts kind of spreading of the gospel, "continuing daily with one accord in the temple, and breaking bread from house to house" (Acts 2:46 NKJV). People begin to bring everyone they know to church, and the contagious atmosphere spreads into the families of all who are converted. This is happening today in many life-giving churches.

Authentic Revival

Revival is characterized by widespread repentance and broken-ness. Religious people suddenly become deeply convinced of their lost state, even though they have been in church for years. They realize that their "Christianity" was merely church attendance and Christian jargon. Now, however, they are deeply convicted of sin and their separation from God. They begin to desire a true rela-tionship with Jesus. Often they will become angry that they were never converted at their previous church, but because of anemic messages and the approval of their worldliness from the pulpit, they never saw a need for the lordship of Christ. Millions of church attendees are yet to be converted to a real, personal relationship with Christ Jesus.

When religious people experience this newfound faith, they find joy and peace. Happiness is the expression on each face. Love per-meates the church, and a burden for the lost and needy is a reality for the first time. Church members begin to look beyond the four walls of the church to the fields of harvest on the outside. They desire to become laborers in that harvest as the Holy Spirit opens their eyes to the needs of people in the community.

When this happens, enthusiasm for God's Word soars and the Bible comes alive for people. People hang upon every word that is preached. There are phenomenal increases in the sales of Bibles. Those who are used of God to bring about revival receive far more calls to preach than they can answer. They become national spiri-tual leaders in a short period of time.

When we go back to the Great Commission and are determined to preach the gospel to every creature and make disciples, we will experience growth in every church. The ceiling of growth is different for every church and every city, but growth will occur. Preach the gospel and give people a life-giving, life-altering experience at your church and watch them come. Where there is life, people abound.

Bring Your Stuff

David, my teenage grandson, is a great baseball player. At the beginning of the 2007 season, I went to watch David play ball. One of his younger brothers, Joseph, was also playing ball that day. Joseph is autistic and plays with the special-needs children. Having had three daughters, I've never had the opportunity to go see "my boys" play baseball. So I was thrilled to go to David's game.

As David's team came out, I noticed a lack of enthusiasm—the players dragged themselves onto the field. David played right field and on one play the ball was hit in his direction. He ran for the ball, but the ball soared over his head. Then he came to bat. I watched with anticipation for David to hit the ball over the fence. You see, at the championship game in 2006, David hit two home runs to lead his team to win the title.

But on this day, it was not to be. His first at-bat, David struck out. He kind of dragged his bat around and threw it toward the dugout and acted as if it was no big deal. Next time at bat, the same thing happened. Again, David showed little emotion as he walked away.

At this I became just a little bit angry. I did not come to this ball-park to watch my grandson lollygag around. I was disappointed that such a fine athlete would not put his heart into the game. I left.

At another field in the same ballpark, my ten-year-old grandson, Joseph, was playing. I went to that field, sat down, and watched Joseph play. Just before the game was over, David came walking up. "Pa, where did you go?" he asked with a playful shove. "I hit a triple."

"Really?" I said. "You struck out the first two times at bat, and you acted like you didn't care."

David seemed a little frustrated and said again, "Pa, but I hit a triple and you didn't see it! Where were you?"

"David, I came to watch Joseph. He really wants to play and puts his heart in it, but you don't. I am not going to watch you drag around and act like you don't care and only play at half of your potential."

He hung his head like a rejected puppy, very upset and disappointed.

"Let's go eat lunch," I told him. "We need to talk." So we went to Wendy's, and of course I let him order anything that he wanted. He liked that!

"David," I said, "if you want to win at life, you're going to have to bring your stuff. You can't expect to accomplish anything meaningful if you don't give it 100 percent. Today, you didn't bring your stuff. Do you know what your stuff is?"

"No, sir," he answered.

So I explained it to him this way: "*S* stands for strength. You have physical strength, mental strength, emotional strength, and spiritual strength. If you don't bring your strength with you, you will eventually fail. And by the way, anyone who is not strong spiritually is not strong at all.

"*T* stands for talent. David, God has given you gifts and talent, and He expects you to use those talents for Him. In whatever you do, you must use what God has given you, or you will not reach your full potential. The worst thing in the world is wasted talent.

"*U* stands for undying commitment to success and excellence. The difference between success and failure is your commitment to reach your goals. Excellence in everything you do will guarantee success.

"*F* stands for focus. You were not focused on the game today. I don't know what you were thinking about, but it wasn't how you could help the team succeed. Without focus and concentration, you will allow everything else to get in the way of your success.

"The final *F* is fun. David, you were not having fun because you did not bring your stuff. And because you were not having fun, I was not having fun."

Then I asked, "So, what are you going to do?"

He looked at me with a huge grin on his face and said, "Pa, the next time I'm gonna bring my stuff!"

When he got home he told his mother, "Mama, Pa took me to lunch and told me some really awesome stuff." That's what grandpas are for.

About a week later during one of his games, I was at home in South Carolina and my daughter Tammy called me. "Dad, David just came up to the fence by the dugout and rattled it and said, 'Mama, call Pa. Tell him that I'm bringing my stuff today!'"

David went on that season to make the All-Star Team. He brought his stuff the rest of the season! While I'm bragging, his brother Jonathan also made All-Stars that year. It's genetics!

Bring Your Stuff to Church

Can you recall when you preached on Sunday morning and you knew you didn't bring your stuff that day? You played golf, went fishing, and surfed the Web that week, but you left your best at home on Sunday. What about in a counseling session with a troubled soul, or the last time you hung out with your wife or children? What about last week's small group? Did you try to breeze through it, forgetting to prepare? Did you forget about pre-*prayer*? You must be 100 percent committed to bring your church to the place where God wants it to be.

This is a very critical time in the history of our country. There are too many distractions, too many problems, too many issues with family and work. We can't afford *not* to bring our stuff every time we are called upon to minister. This book covers several principles and practices that will help us build dynamic attractional churches, and each one requires that we bring to the table all God has given us. We must bring our stuff.

The pastors in this book excel in many (though naturally not all) areas. We're all learning and growing, continually improving. And as we do, we should ask God to help us bring our best—to achieve His Great Commission for His glory.

In the State of Stuck

I am a college football fan. I love the esprit de corps, the sense of "our team," and the intensity of the fans. When the home team wins a big game, we all hold up that pointer finger and cry, "We are number one!"

But what happens when the team slides down that slippery

slope of consecutive losses? We are ready to fire the coach, change quarterbacks, and start all over with a new team.

In October 2007, for the first time in decades, the Irish of Notre Dame had lost their first five games of the season, scoring a total of only 13 points in the first three! The Fighting Irish were 119th in the NCAA in points per game and total yards rushing per game. They were the only 1-A team with no offensive touchdowns to their credit after their third game. They lost to USC in their last regular season game and then were beaten in the postseason bowl game.

The slide started at the end of the 2006 season with that loss to USC. Then came the loss to LSU in the Sugar Bowl. The Bengal Tigers from Cajun land destroyed the Irish 41–14. (For the record, I bleed purple and gold. Geaux Tigers!) Unfortunately, it didn't end there. After decades of dominance, Notre Dame ended the 2007 season with a 3–9 record and a subpar 6–6 record in 2008. It seemed that Notre Dame was in the state of stuck.

When you're down like Notre Dame, it is hard to bring your stuff. People in this situation feel as if they have no stuff left. Maybe that is how you feel. Are you down and discouraged, with little hope of recovering? Are you tired of trying everything you know and still languishing in the losing bracket?

Change is the prerequisite of improvement, and urgency is the beginning of change. Let your discouragement and disappointment create a deep sense of urgency that will drive you to overcome the state of feeling stuck. Be determined to climb out of the rut with new ideas and a new hope.

The process starts when you bring the stuff God has put in your heart, including the vision He imparted to you and the gifts the Holy Spirit has given you. Then change is demanded. You cannot continue to do the same things you've always done in hopes that the same actions will yield different results.

Be willing to say, "It's not working. I'm ready to change everything I am doing in order to fulfill the call of God on my life. I am not too old, too stubborn, or too entrenched in the status quo. I'm willing to do whatever it takes, one more time." The under-churched are waiting for a life-giving church. They very well may be waiting for *you*.

Read and reread this book. Each time you do, ideas will come to you. Call some attractional church pastors and get their input. Implement those ideas and you will regain momentum.

With God's Word and His power, you can do it. Set your heart to reach the lost, the absent, and the unfulfilled, and restore an underchurched world to vibrant life.

Note: After forty-five years of existence, the New Orleans Saints won Super Bowl XLIV! They brought their stuff.

Planting an Attractional Church

Perhaps the ultimate outreach is planting a new church. Whether your church has grown to the size that it needs a new "pot" in which to spread its roots or you discern a call to minister to a specific group in a specific location, church planting may be the next step for your ministry.

One of the greatest joys of my life is church planting. It always involves a young couple who have a dream to move to some U.S. city and start a new church. The process usually takes a year or more, and during that time my partners in ARC become very close and attached to these couples. Training, assessments, and funding these church planters have become our primary activities at ARC.

The process starts and ends with a vision for transforming a city by spiritually impacting the people in each place we go. The energy that goes into launching a new church is enormous, but the payoff is even greater. Thousands of souls are coming to Christ each year as a result of the churches that we have planted.

Since 2001 ARC has planted more than two hundred churches around the country. Each of these teams received the same instruction: "This will be an intense, life-transforming journey. Learn how to pray." The reason is simple: Church planting is a spiritual work. It is a journey defined not just by its pastor or the number of people who attend, but by the spiritual impact it makes on its city. And to make an impact spiritually you must pray and teach those you disciple to pray. Prayer is the "air war" that clears the way for the "ground war." You must clear the resistance with prayer before you can establish a work in your city that will be successful.

The following points are part of the training that we give our church planters at our Church Planting 1.0. This event is available online at www.churchplanter.tv.

Win the War in the Spiritual

Church began with prayer:

> On the day of Pentecost all the believers were meeting together in one place. Suddenly, there was a sound from heaven like the roaring of a mighty windstorm, and it filled the house where they were sitting. Then, what looked like flames or tongues of fire appeared and settled on each of them. And everyone present was filled with the Holy Spirit and began speaking in other languages, as the Holy Spirit gave them this ability (Acts 2:1–4 NLT).

The church was birthed while the original 120 believers were in an upper room praying. Jesus had told the disciples to wait in Jerusalem until the Holy Spirit would come Acts 1:4. Though Scripture doesn't specifically say they were having a prayer meeting, I am sure they were together seeking God for what He had next. And what He had next was powerful. God was about to put fuel into their spiritual tanks by sending the Holy Spirit. Planting a church without prayer is like trying to start a car without first putting in gasoline. It takes energy, the Holy Spirit, and prayer.

Never underestimate the power of prayer and fasting. This is a lesson Pastor Chris Hodges learned in Bogotá, Colombia, with Pastor César Fajardo. "You must win the war in the spiritual," César said repeatedly. César had a cell group program that was sweeping Bogotá with hundreds of groups that were reaching thousands of people…especially young people. Chris flew in from Bethany World Prayer Center in Louisiana and wanted to know typical things like what a cell group looked like, how long it lasted, and how often it met. César would say, "You Americans just don't understand! It's not our program, it's prayer! You must win the war in the spiritual first!"

The same is true for planting a church. Though we have an entire process for preparing church planters to launch a great church, we know that prayer is the real key to their success. Jerry Falwell, founder of Thomas Road Baptist Church, would often say, "Nothing of eternal importance or significance happens apart from prayer."

As pastor, you are the spiritual architect of your church. Whether you are pastor of a new church or one that has been in existence for a hundred years, prayer is still the most important activity you can be involved in. It takes prayer to launch and to build. If you will develop a culture of prayer in your church, you will immediately see that God will begin to move in your life and meetings.

How do you start? Begin with corporate prayer one day per week, like from 8 to 9 on Saturday mornings. Then try a three-day fast with water and fruit juices (urge participants to consult a doctor before undertaking any fast). Then work up to longer periods of prayer and fasting. We found prayer and fasting most strategic at the beginning of each year and in August, just before the two most evangelistic times of the year for our churches. A must-read on the subject of fasting is Bill Bright's book on the subject, *Seven Steps to Successful Fasting and Prayer*.

The critical question you must ask: *Am I winning the battle in the spiritual?*

Teamwork Makes the Dream Work

No matter the size of the church you desire to build, you will need to put much effort into building your team. Your team will make you or break you.

The Launch Team

We call the group that helps start the church the "launch team." The launch team is different from the core group because many of the launch team members will eventually move on. It's like scaffolding that you use to build a building. When you need scaffolding, it is invaluable to the building process. But when you're done building, you take the scaffolding down and move it to the next job. So your original group is a launch team, not a core group. Your core group will be the people who stay with you for a long period of time and have specific roles in the church.

Therefore, it is important not to give anyone expectations for employment when they join your launch team. Wait until you have had some experience with each one before offering positions, especially the paid ones.

Select your relationships carefully because they will determine whether you reach your potential. Complainers, people who don't like to work, and those who have their own agendas will undermine the church plant. Find people who add value to the new church as well as to the other members of the team. Realize up front that each person is like an ingredient in a stew: He or she can make it savory and satisfying or ruin the whole pot. Let leadership rise to the top.

When building the team, we ask ourselves, *Is there a divine flow with those we've chosen?* What do I mean by "divine flow"? When you meet someone with a similar vision and you feel God has brought him into your life for a particular purpose, you are experiencing divine flow. These are people you will do life with.

Here are some qualities to look for:

- Potential value—they have undeveloped abilities. They are people you can develop.
- Positive value—they raise the morale of you and your church. They are happy people who add value to the organization.
- Personal value—you have a relational connection with them. This is a new friend or colleague who makes you better at what you do.
- Production value—they can get things done and they lift the team. One of my favorite quotes is: "Nothing is impossible for the man who does not have to do it himself."

What does the launch team do? It will first of all help you develop your vision and make your vision easy to articulate. Then, as a team, you will determine where you should be located, your purpose, your strategy, and the target group you will focus on. Once these are established, the team will help you determine worship and teaching style.

Finally, they will begin to put together a plan for the launch. Each member will determine a course of action for each week and how the church will be marketed to the community. Then, as each one finds his or her place in the church, people will be recruited to be a part of the teams in each department.

Leadership is ultimately about creating a way for people to contribute to making something extraordinary happen. As a leader, you can help people find their purposes in God's kingdom.

How to Build a Team

Here is how I have built teams over the past thirty years of ministry: Recruit, Embrace, Equip, Empower, Replicate. Let's look at each one.

Recruit

One definition of *recruit* is "to renew, reinvigorate, increase energy, and infuse new blood."[1] Recruiting is, in essence, helping people find a place to serve that fits their gift mix. Then, as they use their gifts in actual service to the church, they bring energy and help invigorate the church as it grows.

Embrace

To embrace means to accept and support willingly and enthusiastically. Once you recruit someone, treat this person as an integral and important part of the endeavor. Don't let team members feel as if they are being exploited or taken advantage of. Appreciate and involve them.

Equip

The best way to add value to team members is to equip them in the specific areas they will be serving in. Whether you train them or someone else on the team does it, a team member always appreciates this help.

Empower

To empower is to give someone the authority to do something. Once you have had time to build rapport and a strong relational bond with team members, it is time to empower them. After they have been recruited, embraced, and equipped, release your team to do what they are ready to do. This is giving them not only the responsibility but the authority to do their tasks, under your leadership and within the boundaries predetermined by others. Once your team members take ownership, they will do great things for the church.

Replicate

To replicate is simply to reproduce or make copies of the original. The job of all team members is to reproduce themselves in new members. Once this process starts, the team will grow and provide an ever-increasing foundation for growth and future expansion.

The critical question to ask yourself: *Do I have the right people on my team?*

Find the Right Location

Here are some criteria for determining whether the location you've chosen is the best.

Visibility

Is the location visible? Does everyone know where it is located? Often a movie theater is located on a side street, but everyone in town knows where it is. The same is true of most high schools— they may be tucked away somewhere, but everyone knows their locations.

Accessibility

Is the location easy to get into and out of? People don't like to fight opposing traffic, make U-turns, or have to wait for long periods of time to get into or out of a parking lot.

Size

Make sure your venue is the correct size. You want to create critical mass, which is the minimum number of people it takes to maintain a sense of being full without seeming crowded (i.e., 65–80 percent full). It shouldn't be too small or too large; auditoriums that seat three hundred to five hundred are normally ideal.

Cost

Limit the cost of your venue to 35 percent of your entire budget. Anything more eats into salaries and other expenses such as outreach and advertising.

Potential for Growth

Will the venue you're looking at allow you to grow? Some of our church planters have signed long-term leases only to outgrow them in a short period of time. Try to stay mobile—use spaces temporarily—for three to five years or until you find the perfect space. The top places to meet include schools, art theaters, and movie theaters.

Take care of the venue, keep it clean, make improvements—bless the people responsible for maintaining the place or whose area you use.

The critical question you should ask yourself: *Is my venue visible and the right size for my launch?*

It Takes Big Money to Plant a Church

The average church plant takes $75,000 to $150,000 to launch. Give careful attention to your fund-raising and budgeting. You should plan on spending most of your launch budget on the first service. Some planters make the mistake of holding back money in case they don't draw enough people after the first month to pay the bills. Instead of spending the money to make sure there would be enough people, they cut back on marketing. The results are normally a small launch.

Use the money you raise to launch large. Launching small has many inherent problems. We recommend aiming for two hundred minimum at the first service and three hundred in attendance in two years minimum, and to be self-supporting.

Where Does the Money Come From?

Money can come from other churches, relatives, businesspeople, savings, home equity, friends, and retirement plans. Just share your vision enthusiastically and be ready to communicate the vision to many people.

Here are some of the reasons people should invest in your church plant:

- Life-giving local churches are the best investments on earth. They reproduce leaders and life that touch the world.
- Life-giving churches reproduce themselves in the form of planting other churches and they invest in world missions.
- It is a statistical fact that a new church will win more souls per capita than an existing church.[2] Souls are always the best investment.
- Life-giving churches give you a good return on your investment because of the way they invest tithes and offerings. They are good stewards of all that God provides through the membership of the church.

Other Financial Matters

Stewardship

Being a good steward of the resources that God provides through giving members is paramount in the eyes of members and others looking to invest in a new church plant. It is necessary to have a stewardship plan and for you to be able to communicate that to those who would invest in your church plant. A great resource for building a stewardship strategy is www.thechangegroup.tv.

Generosity

You need to be generous with people in the church and people in need. Be willing to provide all things that are purchased with offerings at no cost to the members. This includes CDs of messages, T-shirts, special events, refreshments, and special speakers and seminars.

Return on Investment

ROI refers to making sure that the money coming into the church provides the best possible ministry to the families in the church, to the reproduction of its ministries through church planting, and to the reproduction of leaders around the world. As churches and leaders are reproduced with these church finances, those new churches create a source of income that keeps the resources in a multiplying cycle.

Margin

Margin is simply a space before you reach your limits. Like margins on a sheet of writing paper or that extra gallon or two in your gas tank when the low fuel light comes on, margin keeps you from going over the limit. One way you can ensure that there is margin is to base your next year's budget on 90 percent of the previous year's income. This way you start off with a margin of 10 percent.

If you bring in more than last year's income, that adds to your margin.

Then set a budget that strictly adheres to the following percentages:

Salaries: 35 percent
Building: 35 percent
Missions and church planting: 10 percent
Ministry and outreach: 20 percent

If you maintain a margin, there is a great chance that you will never have financial problems. With margin and good stewardship you will have money for missions, expansion, and emergencies. What is best, though, is that the businesspeople in your church will respect you and want to give more.

Budget

In this economy people are especially aware of waste and unnecessary expenses. They will reject any excessive spending by the leadership. Learn to be modest and stay within the budget set each year by the trustees of your church.

Givers

Understand that givers don't like to pay the bills, and they don't respond well to guilt or negativism. Givers also aren't necessarily moved by need—or the neediest churches would have all the money. Givers respond to vision. They want to be a part of something big. So cast a big vision to draw in the monies you need to create your attractional church.

The goal is to launch large, set a budget with built-in margin, and create a resource-rich environment. This means you always have enough to accomplish what God wants you to do without being in debt or financially strained.

The critical question to ask yourself: *Am I using the resources God has provided in the best way?*

Marketing Your New Church

To launch large, you must be intentional about advertising your church to the community. Like it or not, our society depends on marketing for information about new things. A strategic plan for informing the community that you are in town will ensure that on launch Sunday you will have many people in attendance. From word of mouth to massive mail-outs, marketing will let people know that a new church is in town. Great ideas must be marketed or they go unnoticed by the very ones that would benefit from them most.

A Plan for Marketing Your New Church

1. Determine your target audience.
2. Create a relevant marketing strategy.
   - *Direct mail.* It should be only a small part: twice per year.
   - *Advertising.* This includes viral marketing and social networks.
   - *Relational meetings.* These should be face-to-face.
   - *Prelaunch events and services.* Consider things like gasoline giveaways, "bikes or bust" (collecting bicycles for grade-school students), "Servolution" by Dino Rizzo (service projects to the community), and so on.
3. Maintain a continual presence in the community.
   - *Stand out.* What will be your distinctive?
   - *Vision x 1000.* This is when everyone in the church is talking about the new church with a positive tone. It is not just the pastor sharing the vision, but every member of the church repeating it.
   - *Think visibility.* How visual are you?
   - *Momentum.* What can you do to get and keep momentum?

It is vitally important that you get the word out about your new church. Even as expensive as marketing with mail-outs and community outreach may be, over time the few people you gain from these tools will give back many times more than what you spend.

If people don't know you are there, they won't come. This is not the place to be tight financially.

A critical question to ask yourself: *What am I going to do to let my city know that we are here?*

The Wow Factor

You've heard that you never get a second chance to make a first impression. People come expecting little, so wow them! Make a huge impression! Make your first Sunday and every Sunday afterward days they will remember in a positive way.

From the second they enter your parking lot, guests begin forming impressions of your ministry. Successful churches understand that how they appear to people matters. Be refreshingly different. People should get the sense right away that this is something better than their last church experience.

1. Know why people avoid church.
   - The services are boring and too long.
   - The members are unfriendly or there is conflict.
   - The church just wants my money or misuses money.
   - What will happen with my kids? Is it really safe there?
2. Impress them within the first ten minutes in everything from helpful parking attendants to welcoming greeters. High touch and fun/laughter: when people are engaged by members of the church with a smile and helpful gestures.
3. Put your energy and resources into great praise and worship.
4. Children's ministry should be well staffed, safe, clean, and fun.
5. Deliver messages that are interesting, clear, relevant, entertaining, and biblical. Keep asking yourself: *What do I want them to know, and what do I want them to do?* Build messages around your answers.
6. Prayer teams should cover the services behind the scenes to provide a fertile atmosphere for the Holy Spirit to work in.
7. Visitors should be greeted warmly but allowed to remain anonymous.
8. In everything, focus on excellence. It creates comfort.

In a church launch, what is your win? For some it is to have a certain number of visitors and for others it is to have people respond to the message. For most attractional churches it is getting the visitors to come back again and again until they are members. The end result is that they will hear the message of the Bible and eventually accept Christ and become devoted disciples.

The critical question to ask yourself: *What will people talk about on the way home from church?*

Good Church Government

Good church government lays the groundwork for success. Bad church government sows seed of conflict that will sprout later on. Here is what we recommend:

1. Staff leadership in day-to-day ministry matters. You don't want to call the elders every time you need to make a decision in an area such as worship, sermons, schedules, or hiring.
2. Establish internal trustees to manage major financial matters. As pastor, you handle the day-to-day expenses, but appoint trustees to give you insight and wisdom on other major financial transactions, such as leases, notes, and long-term commitments.
3. Establish external overseers to protect and correct the senior pastor in case of immoral behavior, heresy, or the misuse of funds. This way you have shepherds correcting shepherds, not sheep disciplining shepherds. Hurt sheep almost always want revenge instead of correction.

The critical question to ask yourself: *Do I have freedom and accountability?*

Church planting is highly evangelistic and thoroughly biblical. Let these guidelines help you build a team and then a church that attracts the lost, the absent, and the unfulfilled. You can find out more about how the ARC plants churches at www .arcchurches.com.

Twelve Characteristics of the Attractional Church Leader

Characteristic	Its Opposite	How to Foster This Characteristic	How to Diminish This Characteristic
Appreciator leadership style	Tyranny Absolute rule Insecure leadership	Give opportunity and take risks.	Hoard power and authority.
Gift-oriented ministry	Guilt-oriented ministry Random assignments	Trust others with ministry according to their gifts.	Force people to do what you want rather than what they are passionate about.
Passionate spirituality	Religion	Create a culture of excitement and anticipation.	Reinforce how difficult it is to be a passionate believer.
Prayer and fasting	Que sera, sera—what will be, will be	Create a culture of prayer and fasting by being the example.	Devalue fasting and prayer. Avoid spiritual disciplines.
Compassionate, need-oriented evangelism	Confrontational evangelism	Create a "Servolution" culture.	Do evangelism that is confronting, guilt casting, and self-serving.

Characteristic	Its Opposite	How to Foster This Characteristic	How to Diminish This Characteristic
Endurance, tenacity, and perseverance	Resignation Passivity	Press through difficult seasons with optimism.	Change course or quit whenever something is tough.
Functional structures, locations, and logistical arrangements	Functional obsolescence	Strategize to create simple, functional systems. Engage smart people.	Serve with existing outdated structures and avoid strategic planning.
Inspiring worship	Lifeless worship	Engage proven, anointed worship leaders. Worship the way you want your church to worship.	Hold to traditional, outdated forms. Worship out of habit, not out of passion.
Holistic small groups	Avoid small groups	Foster discipleship that focuses on the whole person—body, soul, spirit.	Foster groups that have no spiritual purpose. Ignore the need for smaller discipleship meetings.
Giving and sharing	Self-oriented ministry	Create a culture of generosity.	Focus on getting rather than on giving.
Love and forgiveness	Hate, discord, resentment, blaming	Encourage communication, forgiveness.	Encourage bitterness, holding grudges, cliques, legalism.
Bible-based foundation	Extrabiblical foundation, heresy	Teach from the Bible and use the Bible as your primary playbook.	Avoid using the Bible too much. Focus on popular ideas rather than a biblical foundation.

Vision and Performance Survey

This tool is designed to help church staff and leaders express how they see the church's direction, clarity of vision, and actual performance vs. perceived performance. Use this to facilitate discussion in staff meetings or leadership retreats.

1. If someone were to ask you what the vision of your church or ministry is, what would you tell them?
2. What do you feel your church does best?
3. What do you feel is the number one area where improvement is needed?
4. What aspects of your church would you describe as "life-giving"?
5. What could your church do in Sunday services to be more "attractive"?
6. What things could you do to be more of an "Appreciator" style leader?
7. What would you do to make your church or ministry more relevant?
8. What do you feel is the number one area of ministry that needs critical attention now?

Spend a day discussing the results of this survey with your leadership. Make note of what seems to be a common thread of concern or interest.

The Association of Related Churches

We Plant Life
www.arcchurches.com

ARC is an association of relational churches working with church planters, church leaders, and churches in transition to provide support, guidance, and resources to launch and grow life-giving churches.

Launching Life-Giving Churches

While we recognize and celebrate the unique aspects of every church plant, ARC is committed to supporting a new church's success in four foundational ways:

1. We Help Them Start Strong

We show them how to build their launch team, raise funds, form a worship team, develop their children's ministry and gain momentum—so the new church can open its doors with excellence. If they start strong, they have a greater chance of growing strong.

2. We Reach the Unchurched

With more than 110 million Americans never or rarely attending church, it's critical that we cross cultural walls to reach the lost. ARC is all about helping churches stay culturally relevant—characterized by Bible-based teaching, authentic relationships, and dynamic family ministries.

3. We Build Relationships

Solid relationships are the foundation for growth in any aspect of life. As ARC churches multiply across the country, churches will join an ever-expanding group of people who are committed to one another's success.

4. We Support Financially

Let's face it: churches must have money to gain momentum and keep moving in the right direction. ARC will give a new church the financial push they need to jumpstart its church-planting efforts.

Pastors and Church Leaders

ARC has ready resources for brand-new plants and for churches already under way.

- Conference & Regional Seminars—Besides our annual conference each year, we have several regional events planned throughout the country.
- ARC Resources—Through our resources for ARC partners, a pastor can find sermon series ideas, outlines, PowerPoint presentations, and even video roll-ins.
- Missions—ARC churches have great opportunities for short- and mid-term mission trips.

Notes

One: A Model for Growth

1. David Olson, *The American Church in Crisis,* Zondervan, Copyright 2008, Grand Rapids, MI. Part 1, 21–29.
2. http://www.postkiwi.com/2006/barna-on-small-churches/ & http://www.gallup.com/poll/1597/confidence-institutions .aspx.
3. From: (http://thegospelcoalition.org/blogs/justintaylor/ 2007/03/01/how-many-americans-attend-church-each/). The report says that 83 percent of the citizens of the USA do not attend church regularly...same as David Olsen, author of *The American Church in Crisis*...83 percent of the 309,573,000 population equals 256,945,590 people who do not attend church regularly.
4. http://www.gallup.com/poll/16519/us-evangelicals-how -many-walk-walk.aspx.
5. Suzanne M. Bianchi, John P. Robinson, Melissa A. Milkie, *Changing Rhythms of American Family Life* (New York: Russell Sage Foundation Publishers, September 2007).
6. "Between 2000–2005, that rate is up to 68 percent with average attendance of less than 90 people." http://enrichment journal.ag.org/200904/200904_036_equipping.cfm.

Two: The Calling of Your Church

1. http://www.significantchurch.com.
2. Wikipedia, http://en.wikipedia.org/wiki/Henry_Nott.
3. According to the Hartford Institute for Religion Research: http://hirr.hartsem.edu/research/fastfacts/fast_facts.html#numcong.

Four: First Impressions in the Soybean Field

1. Tony Morgan and Tim Stevens, *Simply Strategic Volunteers: Empowering People for Ministry* (Loveland, CO: Group Publishing, 2005), 67.
2. Gary L. MacIntosh, *Beyond the First Visit* (Grand Rapids: Baker, 2006), 71–72.
3. Brian Bailey, *The Blogging Church: Sharing the Story of Your Church Through Blogs* (San Francisco: Jossey-Bass, 2007), 45.
4. Dale Galloway, *Making Church Relevant* (Kansas City: Beacon Hill Press, 1999), 79.
5. MacIntosh, *Beyond the First Visit*, 34–35, 113.
6. Ibid., 108–10.
7. Kirk Nowery, *The Stewardship of Life: Making the Most of All That You Have and All That You Are* (British Columbia: Spire, 2004), 46.
8. Galloway, *Making Church Relevant*, 82.

Six: The Power of Relationships

1. http://www.substancechurch.com/content/pdf/ProgCell Methods.ARC.pdf. According to the Gallup study, if your "best friend" attends your church, you have a 98 percent chance of being "satisfied" with your church; Michael Lindsay, *Friendship: Creating a Culture of Connectivity in Your Church* (N.P.: Group Publications, 2005), 8.
2. Ibid.
3. Ibid.
4. Will Smith, "Just the Two of Us," *Big Willie Style*, Columbia Records, 1998.
5. *Strong's Exhaustive Concordance*, 1890.

Seven: Meeting God

1. "Outreach Magazine" 2005: "100 Fastest-Growing U.S. Churches" a list by Dr. John N. Vaughan, president and founder of Church Growth Today. Stovall Weems/Celebration Church/Jacksonville, FL ranked #41. June 17, 2005.

Nine: Telling Your Story

1. www.associatedcontent.com/1541809/bible_study_lesson_for _acts_43237.
2. Acts 3:11, 5:12. www.bible-history.com/backd2/solomons_porch .html.

Eleven: Permission Evangelism

1. *Strong's Exhaustive Concordance*, 1890.

Twelve: A Church That Looks Like Jesus

1. Gene Mills, president, PRC Compassion. Used with permission.

Thirteen: Your Church and the Tree of Life

1. Article: Why churches fail, part 1, point 1 by Dr. Richard J. Krejcir. www.ChurchLeadership.org.

Fifteen: Leadership Styles

1. Christian Schwarz, *Natural Church Development: A Guide to Eight Essential Qualities of Healthy Churches* (St. Charles, IL: ChurchSmart Resources, September 1996), 24.
2. www.notablebiographies.com/Ca-Ch | Calvin-John.html.
3. The Breakout Church study by Thom Rainer, 56–57.

Sixteen: Twelve Characteristics of the Attractional Church

1. The information in this section is adapted from *The ABCs of Natural Church Development* by Christian A. Schwarz. Available from ChurchSmart Resources. Once you embrace these characteristics, you can monitor each one with tools that are available at ChurchSmart.com. Used by permission.
2. Christian Schwarz, *Natural Church Development: A Guide to Eight Essential Qualities of Healthy Churches* (St. Charles, IL: ChurchSmart Resources, September 1996).
3. www.edstetzer.com/2009/04/a-denomination-in-decline.html; www.christianitytoday.com/article/decline.in.us.mainline .denominations.continues/25305.htm.
4. *UNChristian* by David Kinnaman and Gabe Lyons...Baker Books, 2007, 181.

Eighteen: A Wonderful Future for Your Church

1. *unChristian: What a New Generation Really Thinks About Christianity...and Why It Matters*, David Kinnaman, The Barna Group, Gabe Lyons, Fermi Project, Baker Books, 2007, 181.
2. See www.pastornet.net.au.

Appendix A: Planting an Attractional Church

1. www.merriam-webster.com/dictionary/recruit.
2. http://www.christianpost.com/article/20100513/total-us -churches-no-longer-in-decline-researchers-say/print.html.

About the Author

Billy Hornsby is a minister that has worked for over thirty years with church leaders nationally and internationally. He is a published author and president of the Association of Related Churches, a nationwide church-planting organization. Billy also serves as the Senior European Consultant for EQUIP, John Maxwell's global leadership training organization. He is a keynote speaker for churches, conferences, and business groups, specializing in topics such as team management, leadership, and how to maintain productive relationships. He has been married for forty-three years to his wife, Charlene.

Other titles by Billy Hornsby include *The Cell Driven Church*, published by Kingdom Publishing, Mansfield, PA, 2000, and *Success for the Second in Command*, published by Creation House, A Strang Company, Lake Mary, FL, 2005.

Social Media

Blog: billyhornsby.com
Twitter: @billyhornsby
Facebook: Billy Hornsby